S0-CDP-006

HF 1416 P7

RETURN TO WAHLQUIST LIBRARY
ALLABLE.

Small Open Economies

Small Open Economies

Their Structure and Policy Environment

Martin F.J. Prachowny
Queen's University

Lexington Books
D.C. Heath and Company
Lexington, Massachusetts
Toronto   London

Library of Congress Cataloging in Publication Data

Prachowny, Martin F.J.
  Small open economies: their structure and policy environment.

  Includes bibliographical references and index.
  1. International economic relations. 2. Economic policy.
3. States, Small. I. Title.
HF1416.P7   382.1   74-25068
ISBN 0-669-97352-1

Copyright © 1975 by D.C. Heath and Company

All rights reserved. No part of this publication may be reproduced or transmitted in any form or by any means, electronic or mechanical, including
photocopy, recording, or any information storage or retrieval system, without permission in writing from the publisher.

Published simultaneously in Canada

Printed in the United States of America

International Standard Book Number: 0-669-97352-1

Library of Congress Catalog Card Number: 74-25068

Dedicated to my parents

Contents

List of Figures

List of Tables

Preface

This study was undertaken during a sabbatical year spent at The University of Michigan. A Leave Fellowship from the Canada Council enabled me to pursue my research interests with a single-mindedness impossible in a normal academic situation. For this assistance I am genuinely grateful. The Research Seminar in International Economics at The University of Michigan, under the direction of Robert M. Stern, provided me the forum for testing my ideas at various stages of the study. For his willingness to suffer intrusions on his own work and for his many valuable suggestions, I am most indebted to Alan V. Deardorff. Steve Kaliski and J. David Richardson have read most of the manuscript and their incisive comments are much appreciated. Mrs. Pat Rapley typed the various drafts of the manuscript with consummate skill. Needless to say, the author cheerfully accepts the responsibility for any shortcomings still imbedded in this study.

Parts of Chapter 4 were previously published in *Weltwirtschaftliches Archiv*. The publishers of this journal have graciously consented to have this material reproduced in this book. Permission to reprint excerpts from Robert A. Mundell's article in the *Canadian Journal of Economics and Political Science* has been granted by the Canadian Political Science Association and the author.

Preface

1

An Introduction to Small Open Economies

The Small Open Economy as an Economic Concept

The small open economy (SOE) is a theoretical abstraction; it is unlikely that a precise empirical counterpart to this concept exists. The SOE possesses no physical dimensions; it has only economic properties. With this in mind, definitions of SOEs based on some maximum size or population, or even on some minimum ratio of trade to Gross National Product, can be eliminated. Rather, an SOE is defined in terms of its economic behavior. A *small open economy* is any country (or other political jurisdiction, for that matter) that treats the price of any internationally traded commodity or asset as exogenously determined and attempts to maximize some objective function with this constraint in mind. The term small refers to the fact that in relation to total world availability of any traded good or asset, the SOE provides only a miniscule fraction. The term open, on the other hand, implies that the tradable sector plays an important role in the structure of the economy. In a sense, an SOE is analogous to a firm in perfect competition that also attempts to maximize an objective function (the objective in this case is to maximize profits) subject to the constraint of given commodity and factor prices.

The economic properties of SOEs and the physical characteristics of small countries may indeed overlap; that is, an SOE as defined here is likely to be small in size and population. While this classification may facilitate the identification of those political entities that might be considered as SOEs, it does not help in elucidating the economic structure of SOEs. In any case, there are likely to be exceptions to the physical dimensions specified for the purpose. For instance, the Soviet Union, which is an economic giant in most respects, is likely to approximate the behavior of an SOE in its trade with Western countries. While it may be able to impose favorable terms of trade in its dealings with bloc countries, the Soviet Union is essentially a price-taker when buying or selling goods in capitalistic markets.[a]

Although the SOE is a theoretical proposition, it is not devoid of

---

[a]See F.D. Holzman[1] and F.L. Pryor[2] who argue that, at least in the 1950s, the Soviet Union faced discrimination by the Western countries. But except for the recent large wheat sales by the United States to the Soviet Union, trade between the Soviet Union and the industrialized countries of the West has rarely affected the world price of the traded commodity.

empirical relevance. There are a large number of countries that more fully satisfy the specifications of an SOE than they do the models of large, or essentially closed, economies—to name just a few: Austria, Belgium, Canada, Denmark, the Netherlands, and New Zealand would seem to fit into this framework quite comfortably. It is true that the post-war period has been a time of coalescence of many countries into opposing power blocs, as well as a time for the establishment of customs unions and other forms of economic integration, causing one to have doubts about the usefulness of the SOE as an economic concept. But there has also been a continuing process of economic and political disintegration, demands for greater local autonomy within existing political jurisdictions, as well as the inability of the European Economic Community to arrive at a viable modality for monetary and fiscal integration. Thus it is important to understand the policy environment of existing and newly emerging political entities, many of which are, for practical purposes, approximations of SOEs.[b]

An SOE is *sui generis*. International trade theory, macroeconomic theory, or balance-of-payments theory based on large countries and their interactions cannot simply be applied to small economic entities. All too often, economists have resorted to economic models relevant to countries such as the United States in analyzing the problems essentially of small open economies, without even mentioning the radical differences in the structure of SOEs and the large economies. This is not to deny that an important segment of the literature has been devoted to the special circumstances faced by SOEs. The pioneers in this area are R.A. Mundell[3] and T.W. Swan.[4] But their work and that which followed in their wake has been far from comprehensive,[c] and it does not seem to have made any significant inroads into the decision-making process of the authorities in those countries that, by their very nature, need not take into account the external repercussions of their policies.

The External Environment

The rest of the world is essentially a closed economy. While the SOE is influenced by events from within its own borders and from abroad, the rest

---

[b]So as not to overemphasize the general applicability of the theory of small open economies, it must be stated that the special problems faced by small, underdeveloped nations will not be dealt with in this study and no relevance for these countries is envisaged.

[c]One exception is P.J. Lloyd.[5] But a major part of his book is devoted to finding a common element for countries that are physically small. He rejects the concept of an SOE as used in this study since he finds the notion of a price-taker to be empirically inconsequential for most small countries. For instance, he asserts that, "Denmark's butter trade constituted 24 percent of the world total and its bacon 94 percent" (p. 41). But these figures do not offer proof that Denmark is not a price-taker in these markets. To do this it would be necessary to show that its excess supply of these two commodities is a significant portion of *total* world demand.

of the world is impervious to external shocks. But what is the economic and political structure of this external environment? Is it one large monolith or is it composed of a large number of SOEs? If the SOE is to be considered as a perfect competitor, does it necessarily imply that the entire world is a network of perfectly competitive markets? Not necessarily. An analogy to the theory of the firm may be helpful. An industry with a few giants and several small firms may not be perfectly competitive, but under many circumstances, the small firms are still forced to act as atomistic competitors. They take for granted the course of action followed by the giants, deciding on their own profit maximizing output and input combinations on the basis of these exogenously given factors. The large firms, in turn, pay little attention to the actions of the small firms.

The SOE may face the same type of environment, but it can still exist and operate efficiently. The only stipulation is that the rest of the world must be benevolent, or at least neutral in its attitude toward the SOE, for if large countries do exist, and if they are malevolent, then the SOE may not be able to survive political, economic, or military pressures. Given its insignificantly small size in economic terms, it makes no sense for any large country to threaten its existence. It cannot be said that an SOE may control the supply of some highly desirable and vital raw material or other commodity not found elsewhere, because this would imply that the SOE had some monopoly power—a self-contradiction. It may be true that one or more of the large countries will find it worthwhile to annex a *number* of SOEs, because as a group they represent a not insignificant economic entity, but each SOE in isolation should still act as if its policies had no external repercussions.

For present purposes, therefore, it is not crucial that the structure of the external environment be specified in any great detail, as long as it is possible for the SOE to exist in this environment, to change its policies as it sees fit, and as long as it has some assurance that the rest of the world remains passive to any events generated within the SOE.

The Scope of the Study

This study is strictly theoretical and abstract in nature. It deals with a hypothetical small open economy. No attempt is made to cope with the practical implications of the analysis for any particular country that may approximate the characteristics of an SOE. Of course, it is possible to apply the generalized theoretical results to a given situation, making due allowances for any special circumstances, both structural and institutional; however, these excursions into the "real" world will have to await more specialized studies.

There are two major objectives of this undertaking. The first is to describe the operation of a smoothly functioning, fully-employed small open economy and to relate some well-known theorems to the special case of an SOE. The second is to provide some conclusions about the effectiveness of the standard macroeconomic policies for dealing with unemployment and inflation—problems afflicting many countries, both large and small.

The structure of the SOE is developed in Chapters 2 and 3. They deal with the special characteristics of the commodity, factor, and asset markets in an SOE. Of special importance is the assumption that if a commodity or asset is traded internationally, then it is indistinguishable from those available in the rest of the world. Because the SOE provides a negligible portion of the total world supply of these homogeneous goods or assets, it is a price-taker in those markets.[d]

The policy models in Chapters 4 and 5 are neither strictly Keynesian nor strictly monetarist in conception. Their aim is to determine the effectiveness of monetary, fiscal, and exchange-rate policies as stabilization instruments in an economy where unemployment is consistent with equilibrium in other markets, but their construction has not precluded *a priori* the effectiveness of either monetary or fiscal policy. However, under some set of circumstances, one or the other policy becomes inoperative. In this regard, the type of exchange-rate system adopted by the SOE is crucial.[e] Chapter 6 deals with the inflationary process peculiar to an SOE. The analysis does not require either a Phillips curve trade-off or a generalized domestic excess demand to generate inflation in the SOE, but instead it relies on inflation being transmitted from the rest of the world. However, the SOE need not accept this externally generated inflation if it is prepared to allow the exchange rate to drift in the appropriate direction.

One of the recurring conclusions from the discussion about policy effectiveness is that flexible exchange rates are invariably superior to fixed exchange rates, a result that reinforces my already strong preference for complete flexibility in the foreign exchange market. The recent conversion of central bankers and politicians to market determined exchange rates as a practical solution to not only payments imbalances but also inflation is in some ways related to the theoretical propositions derived in this study.[f] In particular, it is shown in subsequent chapters that the domestic price level in an SOE is determined to a large extent by the exchange rate and flexibility of that rate allows the authorities to use monetary and fiscal policies to achieve a degree of price stability and full employment not possible if exchange rates are held fixed. (Perhaps the practitioners under-

[d]An overview of the structure of the SOE is provided in the next section.

[e]This important conclusion was first derived by R.A. Mundell.[6]

[f]The conversion to flexibility is not complete as can be seen from the attempts to maintain a system of "managed" floats.

Table 1-1
The Markets in a Small Open Economy

		Price Determined In	
Market	Actors	World Markets	Domestic Markets
Exportables	D, F, (G)	X	
Importables	D, F, (G)	X	
Nontradables	D, (G)		X
Labor	D		X
Land	D		X
Money	D, C	(Not Applicable)	
Bonds	D, F, C	X	

Note: D = domestic residents; F = foreigners; G = government; C = central bank. The parentheses around G implies that the government as a fiscal agent has no role to play except in the case where full employment is not achieved automatically. Money is the numeraire and all other prices are in money terms.

stood these propositions instinctively without requiring an elaborate theoretical model.)

The Structure of an SOE

Before discussion the details of the structure of an SOE, a simple presentation of an overview of the total economy may be useful. The framework for analysis is developed in terms of markets and the actors that take part in them. There are markets for three commodities, two factors, and two assets.[g] By assumption, some markets involve transactions between domestic residents and foreigners, with the latter dictating the equilibrium prices, while other markets involve only transactions among domestic residents allowing the supply and demand conditions in the SOE to determine equilibrium prices. Table 1-1 categorizes the markets in an SOE according to this distinction.

Although it is possible to classify markets on the basis of whether they deal with traded or nontraded goods or assets, it would be erroneous to infer that in those markets where foreign transactions are absent, the domestically determined price has no relationship to the prices of traded goods or assets. For instance, while the two factors of production, labor and land, are assumed to be immobile internationally, their rates of return are determined uniquely by the prices of exportables and importables, as will be shown in Chapter 2.

This classification does not apply to the money market. The price of this numeraire is always one. There is one additional market which does not fit

[g]A third asset, nontraded equities, is briefly considered in Chapter 3.

into this framework—the foreign exchange market. If fixed exchange rates prevail, then the exchange rate (that is, the price of the foreign currency) is determined by decree. Under flexible exchange rates, the rate is market-determined by transactions between domestic residents and foreigners, but the SOE is not strictly a price-taker in this market since it can influence this rate by its actions.

Conclusion

P.J. Lloyd ends his study of small countries by asserting that the approach taken here is rather sterile. He states:

The primary conclusion of this study . . . is that small countries are a heterogeneous group which do not have uniform trade characteristics and cannot be expected to behave in the same way under similar circumstances. . . . Rather than attempt to develop general theories which will relate to all small . . . countries . . . one should consider *for each model* only those countries which do have the characteristics or relationships upon which the model is based. . . . Sound predictive models can be constructed only with particular countries in mind, and the results of these models cannot be extended to other countries which, upon inspection, do not share the same characteristics.[7]

In spite of this pessimistic warning, I intend to proceed on the course charted in this chapter. I remain convinced that a general theory of small open economies offers many useful deductions and conclusions, as well as empirically testable hypotheses. If these hypotheses are refuted by the evidence, this should not tempt one to abandon theorizing, but to improve one's theory.

Notes

1. F.D. Holzman, "Soviet Foreign Trade Pricing and the Question of Discrimination," *Review of Economics and Statistics* 44 (1962): 134-47.

2. F.L. Pryor, *The Communist Foreign Trade System,* Cambridge, Mass., The M.I.T. Press, 1962, Ch. 6.

3. R.A. Mundell, "Capital Mobility and Stabilization Policy Under Fixed and Flexible Exchange Rates," *Canadian Journal of Economics and Political Science* 29 (1963): 475-85; _____ , "A Reply: Capital Mobility and Size," *Canadian Journal of Economics and Political Science* 30 (1964): 421-31.

4. T.W. Swan, "Economic Control in a Dependent Economy," *Economic Record* 36 (1960): 51-66.

5. P.J. Lloyd, *International Trade Problems of Small Nations,* Durham, N.C., Duke University Press, 1968.

6. Mundell, "Capital Mobility and Stabilization Policy," pp. 475-85; "Capital Mobility and Size," pp. 421-31.

7. Lloyd, *International Trade Problems,* p. 127, italics in the original.

2

The Commodity and Factor Markets

Introduction

Any economy, whether large or small, produces and consumes a wide variety of goods and services. For the purposes of this analysis, only three types of final commodities will be considered: exportables, importables, and nontradables. In the production of these commodities, two primary, nontraded and nonreproducible factors in fixed supply, labor and land, are fully employed. These abstractions dictate a three-commodity, two-factor model of international trade. The only deviation from the more standard "two-by-two" model commonly used in international trade theory is the introduction of nontradables. While the analysis could proceed without this third commodity, its incorporation into the model serves a number of useful purposes. As shall be seen later, a small open economy is unable to alter its terms of trade; under these circumstances it will be appropriate to aggregate exportables and importables into a category called tradables that reduces the model to "two-by-two" dimensions. In this case, the nontradable sector is crucial since it serves "as a kind of reservoir which may release factors to the international sector, or absorb factors from that sector, in response to variations in prices."[1] Also, in analyzing policy effectiveness in a small open economy, it will be found that fiscal policy is only effective if it operates in the nontradable sector.

In this chapter, I propose to investigate the micro-economic underpinnings of the commodity and factor markets in a small open economy. The results of this investigation will then be incorporated into the policy models that will be developed in later chapters. However, in making that transition, I will drop some assumptions made in this chapter, namely that full employment prevails under all circumstances or, more generally, that there exists a set of prices that will clear all markets.

Also, since I am abstracting from asset-market equilibrium (a topic to be covered in the next chapter), it is convenient to assume that all income is spent on the three commodities, that the interest rate is not an argument in any of the demand functions, that wealth adjustments, including those through the capital account of the balance of payments, are absent.

In what follows, I will attempt to provide the rationale for the distinction between tradables and nontradables and an operational definition of the small open economy as it relates to commodity markets. These propositions will then be incorporated into a general equilibrium model of the

9

commodity and factor markets of an SOE. Having done that, it is then possible to determine the applicability of some standard theorems in international trade theory.

Definitions of Exportables, Importables, and Nontradables

An open economy is assumed to produce exportables, importables, and nontradables. An industry producing a homogeneous commodity is an exportable industry if any of its output is sold abroad. For this industry, domestic production exceeds domestic consumption at existing world prices. Another industry producing a different homogeneous commodity is an importable industry if any of its output competes with foreign production of that same commodity in the domestic market. For this industry, domestic consumption exceeds domestic production at prevailing world prices. A third industry that neither sells abroad nor competes with foreign production in the home market is a nontradable industry. In this case, domestic production equals domestic consumption and their interaction determines the domestic price of the commodity.

The existence of a nontradable industry, according to M.C. Kemp, is based on "high costs of transport, prohibitive tariffs, export or import embargos based on considerations of defense, international disparities in preferences or in levels of income per capita. . . ."[2] In the absence of these factors, all industries would be exportable or importable industries. In other words, transportation costs, tariffs and other impediments to international trade, usually assumed away for the sake of simplicity and elegance, give rise to industries that, within a relevant range of prices, do not compete in world markets. Kemp estimates that, "In most moderately to heavily industrialized countries the production of domestic or nontraded goods represents more than one-half of total output."[3] Moreover, in advanced countries the fastest growing sectors of the economy are services, both privately and publicly supplied, suggesting a secular decline in the importance of internationally traded goods.

The Small Open Economy as a Price-Taker in World Markets

The assumption that the home country is small in relation to the rest of the world implies that those domestic industries which compete in world markets (that is, exportables and importables) have no market power. Whether the industry has one or many firms, it must act as a perfect competitor if each firm is to maximize its profits. Under these circumstances, the exportable industry faces an infinitely large foreign excess demand elasticity while the importable industry faces an infinite foreign excess supply elasticity. This proposition can be proven in a relatively straightforward manner. For the ith exportable industry there is foreign excess demand, so that

$$D_i^* = A_i^*(p_i) - Q_i^*(p_i) \tag{2.1}$$

while for the jth importable industry there is foreign excess supply written as

$$-D_j^* = Q_j^*(p_j) - A_j^*(p_j) \tag{2.2}$$

where $\quad D_i^*,\, D_j^* =$ foreign excess demand for the ith or jth commodity (a minus sign represents excess supply)

$\quad Q_i^*,\, Q_j^* =$ foreign output of the ith or jth commodity

$\quad A_i^*,\, A_j^* =$ foreign demand for the ith or jth commodity

$\quad p_i,\, p_j =$ equalized domestic and foreign prices of the ith and jth commodities

Differentiating these equations with respect to p_i and p_j respectively, the following elasticities are derived:

$$\eta_{D_i^*,\, p_i} = \eta_{A_i^*,\, p_i} \frac{A_i^*}{D_i^*} - \eta_{Q_i^*,\, p_i} \frac{Q_i^*}{D_i^*} \tag{2.3}$$

$$-\eta_{D_j^*,\, p_j} = \eta_{Q_j^*,\, p_j} \frac{Q_j^*}{D_j^*} - \eta_{A_j^*,\, p_j} \frac{A_j^*}{D_j^*} \tag{2.4}$$

where $\eta_{D_i^*,\, p_i}$ represents the elasticity of D_i^* with respect to p_i, etc. From the assumption that the home country is small in relation to the rest of the world, the excess demands are infinitely small compared with output or demand in the rest of the world. Hence

$$\eta_{D_i^*,\, p_i} \to -\infty \text{ as } \frac{A_i^*}{D_i^*} \to \infty \text{ and } \frac{Q_i^*}{D_i^*} \to \infty$$

$$-\eta_{D_j^*,\, p_j} \to \infty \text{ as } \frac{Q_j^*}{D_j^*} \to \infty \text{ and } \frac{A_j^*}{D_j^*} \to \infty$$

To the extent that only one price prevails in world markets (including the domestic market), domestic producers are constrained to operate as perfect competitors, no matter how few firms there are in the industry. To illustrate this point, assume, for example, that the domestic importable industry is characterized by monopoly conditions. In autarky, the monopolist would set his profit-maximizing price according to

$$p_j \left(1 - \frac{1}{\eta_j} \right) = MC_j \tag{2.5}$$

where η_j is the domestic demand elasticity. However, in a small open economy, he has no control over the world price of the commodity nor over its domestic price. Thus his profit function is

$$\Pi_j = A_j \cdot p_j(A_j) - D_j \cdot p_j(D_j) - C_j(Q_j) \tag{2.6}$$

where A_j and Q_j are total domestic demand and domestic output, respectively and $C_j(\ )$ represents the monopolist's cost function. Since p_j is exogenously determined, the monopolist will follow the rule of

$$p_j = \frac{dC_j}{dQ_j} = MC_j \tag{2.7}$$

which is the same as that for a firm in a perfectly competitive industry. However, depending on the degree of constraint on entry into the industry, the monopolist is able to sustain positive profits even in the long run. A monopolist in the exportable industry can be shown to behave in a similar fashion.

The Distinction Between Tradables and Nontradables

In analyzing the behavior of firms in the exportable and importable industries, it was assumed that only one price prevailed for any homogeneous commodity anywhere in the world. Yet the existence of impediments to trade enumerated above give rise to price differentials between countries and lead to some commodities being nontraded. To make the distinction clearest between exportables and importables on the one hand and non-tradables on the other, it would be most convenient to assume that traded goods are subject to virtually no impediments such as transportation costs or tariffs, while for nontraded goods these impediments are prohibitively large. But in fact there is a continuous spectrum of impediments, and trade takes place in spite of them. To draw the line between traded and nontraded goods is therefore somewhat more complicated. The problem may be analyzed by assuming that *ad valorem* tariffs play the dominant role as impediments to trade, although transportation costs could be substituted for tariffs without altering the results. The important point to note is that tariffs are applied to all three commodities. Assume that the home country is small in that its output or consumption of any commodity relative to another (large) country is infinitely small. Both the small and the large country impose import tariffs.[a] Let p be the domestic (small country) price of a commodity and p^* the price in the large country while τ is the domestic tariff rate and τ^* is the foreign tariff rate.

For an industry to be classified as an importable in the domestic country, it must be true that at the equilibrium price relationship of $p^*(1 + \tau) = p$, domestic demand exceeds domestic supply. On the other hand, for an industry to be considered an exportable, domestic output must exceed domestic demand at $p^* = p(1 + \tau^*)$. For an industry to be a nontradable, it must be true that when $p < p^*(1 + \tau)$ and $p^* < p(1 + \tau^*)$, neither exports nor imports take place. The dividing lines among the three different types of industries is shown in Figure 2-1.

For any particular commodity, the interaction of supply and demand in the large country determines the world price. This in turn establishes maximum and minimum prices in the home country. Given τ and τ^*, the price can go no higher than $p^*(1 + \tau)$ because of the limitless supply of imports at that price, and no lower than $p^*[1/(1 + \tau^*)]$ because the home country can sell all it wants at that price. For a given demand curve in the home country, three supply curves have been drawn, each one giving rise to a different situation. (Alternatively, the supply curve could be held fixed and three different demand curves could be drawn. The end result would be the same.)

If S_1 is the relevant supply curve, the equilibrium domestic price is $p = p^*(1 + \tau)$, where domestic output is Q_1 and domestic demand is A_1. Since $A_1 > Q_1$, this industry is an importable and imports are equal to $A_1 - Q_1$. If, on the other hand, S_3 is the relevant supply curve, then the equilibrium price in the domestic market is $p = p^*[1/(1 + \tau^*)]$ with domestic output being Q_3 and domestic demand equal to A_3. The amount $Q_3 - A_3$ is exported indicating that this is an exportable industry. Lastly, if S_2 is the supply curve, domestic demand and supply by themselves interact to determine the domestic price at p_2. This establishes the industry as a nontradable. The dotted supply curves S_4 and S_5 provide the dividing lines among the three types of goods with S_4 being the boundary between an importable and a nontradable and S_5 dividing nontradables from exportables.

The main factors influencing these divisions are: (1) domestic and foreign tariffs or other impediments to trade, and (2) the autarky equilibrium price in the home country in relation to the world equilibrium price. All other things being equal, the higher are tariffs or other impediments, the larger is the range between the maximum and minimum prices in the home country and the more nontraded goods there will be. Raising the domestic

[a]Tariffs on the exported commodity are redundant and are omitted from further consideration. Domestic taxes and subsidies on tradables and nontradables will be analyzed in the section, "The Effect of Taxes and Subsidies on Relative Prices."

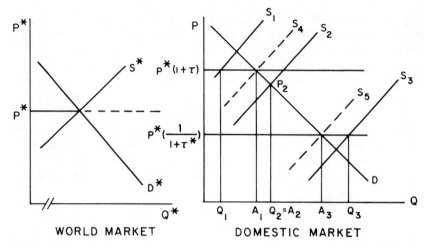

Figure 2-1. The Determination of Tradable and Nontradable Commodities

tariff will increase the likelihood of the importable becoming a nontradable and raising the foreign tariff sufficiently will convert the exportable industry into a nontradable. At the same time, for any given level of tariffs, the higher the autarky price relative to the world price of a commodity, the more likely it is an importable, while the opposite is true for an exportable commodity. This is simply an expression of the theory of comparative advantage after demand conditions have been taken into account.

To summarize, the domestic price of exportables and importables are determined in world markets and in the absence of changes in τ and τ^* there is a linear relationship between changes in world and domestic prices. On the other hand, the domestic price of nontradables is determined by domestic demand and supply conditions, but only if exogenous changes in these conditions leave the equilibrium price within the range established by the maximum and minimum prices. In the remainder of this study, a number of exogenous changes in the system will be treated and it is well to keep in mind that these changes must be small enough in relation to that range for the nontradable industry to remain in that category and not to shift to the exportable or importable industries.

A General Equilibrium Model of the Commodity and Factor Markets

Having made the crucial distinction between tradable and nontradable commodities and having provided the rationale for the assumption that a small open economy treats the price of tradables (that is, exportables and importables) as exogenous, it is now convenient to incorporate these conclusions into a general equilibrium model of such an economy. The main purpose of the model is to investigate some of the basic theorems in international trade theory in the face of the small country assumptions.

For this investigation, R.W. Jones's exposition of a general equilibrium model[4] is ideally suited. The main alternations to his model will be the introduction of a third, nontraded commodity and the exogeneity of the prices of the two traded commodities. Although Ryutaro Komiya[5] has already incorporated nontraded goods into a model of international trade, his analysis only infrequently makes reference to a *small* open economy.

The Production Sector

The small open economy is assumed to produce three commodities: exportables (Q_x), importables (Q_m), and nontradables (Q_n). There are two primary factors of production in fixed supply: labor (L) and land (T). The domestic prices of goods are p_x, p_m, and p_n for exportables, importables, and nontradables, respectively. Foreign prices of exportables and importables are p_x^* and p_m^*. Any divergences between domestic and foreign prices are dictated by the domestic tariff on importables (τ_m) and the foreign tariff on exportables (τ_x^*). The return to labor is the wage rate (w) and the return to land is rent (r). The exchange rate, expressed as the price of the foreign currency, is π. The essential equations of the production side of the model are as follows:

$$a_{Lx}Q_x + a_{Lm}Q_m + a_{Ln}Q_n = L \tag{2.8}$$

$$a_{Tx}Q_x + a_{Tm}Q_m + a_{Tn}Q_n = T \tag{2.9}$$

$$a_{Lx}w + a_{Tx}r = p_x \tag{2.10}$$

$$a_{Lm}w + a_{Tm}r = p_m \tag{2.11}$$

$$a_{Ln}w + a_{Tn}r = p_n \tag{2.12}$$

$$p_x = \pi p_x^* \left(\frac{1}{1 + \tau_x^*} \right) \tag{2.13}$$

$$p_m = \pi p_m^* (1 + \tau_m) \tag{2.14}$$

The a_{ij}'s describe the technology in the production of the three commodities. Specifically, a_{ij} is the quantity of factor i ($i = L, T$) required for the production of a unit of Q_j ($j = x, m, n$). It represents the *inverse* of the average product of each factor in the production function of each commodity In the case of variable proportions, a_{ij} depends only on the ratio of factor returns.

Equations (2.8) and (2.9) stipulate that the supply of both factors is exhausted by the demand for these factors in the production of the three commodities. Equations (2.10), (2.11) and (2.12) indicate that the domestic price of each commodity is determined by unit costs in a competitive equilibrium with constant returns to scale. The last two equations stipulate that the domestic prices of the first two commodities are determined by their world prices, the relevant tariff rates and the exchange rate.[b]

Holding only τ_m and τ_x^* constant, we can derive the equations of change where ($\hat{\ }$) represents the proportional change in a variable (e.g., $\hat{Q}_x = dQ_x/Q_x$).

$$\lambda_{Lx}\hat{Q}_x + \lambda_{Lm}\hat{Q}_m + \lambda_{Ln}\hat{Q}_n = \hat{L} - [\lambda_{Lx}\hat{a}_{Lx} + \lambda_{Lm}\hat{a}_{Lm} + \lambda_{Ln}\hat{a}_{Ln}] \quad (2.15)$$

$$\lambda_{Tx}\hat{Q}_x + \lambda_{Tm}\hat{Q}_m + \lambda_{Tn}\hat{Q}_n = \hat{T} - [\lambda_{Tx}\hat{a}_{Tx} + \lambda_{Tm}\hat{a}_{Tm} + \lambda_{Tn}\hat{a}_{Tn}] \quad (2.16)$$

$$\theta_{Lx}\hat{w} + \theta_{Tx}\hat{r} = \hat{p}_x - [\theta_{Lx}\hat{a}_{Lx} + \theta_{Tx}\hat{a}_{Tx}] \quad (2.17)$$

$$\theta_{Lm}\hat{w} + \theta_{Tm}\hat{r} = \hat{p}_m - [\theta_{Lm}\hat{a}_{Lm} + \theta_{Tm}\hat{a}_{Tm}] \quad (2.18)$$

$$\theta_{Ln}\hat{w} + \theta_{Tn}\hat{r} = \hat{p}_n - [\theta_{Ln}\hat{a}_{Ln} + \theta_{Tn}\hat{a}_{Tn}] \quad (2.19)$$

$$\hat{p}_x = \hat{p}_x^* + \hat{\pi} \quad (2.20)$$

$$\hat{p}_m = \hat{p}_m^* + \hat{\pi} \quad (2.21)$$

Jones points out that the λ's and θ's are transforms of the a_{ij}'s in equations (2.8) to (2.12). Specifically, $\lambda_{Lx} = a_{Lx}Q_x/L$ is the fraction of the total labor force employed in the exportable industry and $\theta_{Lx} = a_{Lx}[w/p_x]$ is labor's share in the exportable industry.

In matrix form, I define

$$\lambda = \begin{bmatrix} \lambda_{Lx} & \lambda_{Lm} & \lambda_{Ln} \\ \\ \lambda_{Tx} & \lambda_{Tm} & \lambda_{Tn} \end{bmatrix} \quad \text{and} \quad \theta = \begin{bmatrix} \theta_{Lx} & \theta_{Tx} \\ \theta_{Lm} & \theta_{Tm} \\ \theta_{Ln} & \theta_{Tn} \end{bmatrix}$$

From the definitions of the λ's and θ's, each row in the λ and θ matrices adds to unity. Henceforth, assume that the exportable industry is labor-intensive relative to the importable industry and that the importable industry is land-intensive relative to the exportable industry. The factor intensity

---

[b]An inequality could also be derived for the domestic price of Q_n such that p_n is bounded by πp_n^* $(1 + \tau_n)$ and πp_n^* $1/(1 + \tau_n^*)$.

of the nontradable industry relative to the other two commodities will not be specified at this stage of the analysis. As a result of the factor-intensity assumptions, it follows that the proportion of the labor force in the exportable industry (λ_{Lx}) divided by the proportion of the land used in that industry (λ_{Tx}) exceeds the proportion of land used in the importable industry (λ_{Lm}) divided by the proportion of labor in the same industry (λ_{Tm}). Also labor's share in the exportable industry (θ_{Lx}) exceeds labor's share in the importable industry (θ_{Lm}). Now partition the λ and θ matrices, so that

$$\lambda' = \begin{bmatrix} \lambda_{Lx} & \lambda_{Lm} \\ \\ \lambda_{Tx} & \lambda_{Tm} \end{bmatrix} \qquad \theta' = \begin{bmatrix} \theta_{Lx} & \theta_{Tx} \\ \\ \theta_{Lm} & \theta_{Tm} \end{bmatrix}$$

from which

$$|\lambda'| = \lambda_{Lx}\,\lambda_{Tm} - \lambda_{Tx}\,\lambda_{Lm} > 0$$

and

$$|\theta'| = \theta_{Lx} - \theta_{Lm} > 0$$

If the factor-intensity assumption is reversed, then $|\lambda'| < 0$ and $|\theta'| < 0$.

R.W. Jones has also proven[6] that for both fixed and variable proportions

$$\theta_{Lj}\,\hat{a}_{Lj} + \theta_{Tj}\,\hat{a}_{Tj} = 0 \tag{2.22}$$

for $j = x, m, n$. Defining the elasticity of factor substitution as

$$\sigma_j = \frac{\hat{a}_{Tj} - \hat{a}_{Lj}}{\hat{w} - \hat{r}} \tag{2.23}$$

for $j = x, m, n$, provides us with three additional equations that together with the three equations of (2.22) can be solved for the $\hat{a}_{ij}$'s. Substituting these values into equations (2.15) and (2.16), the result is

$$\lambda_{Lx}\hat{Q}_x + \lambda_{Lm}\hat{Q}_m + \lambda_{Ln}\hat{Q}_n = \hat{L} + \delta_L(\hat{w} - \hat{r}) \tag{2.24}$$

$$\lambda_{Tx}\hat{Q}_x + \lambda_{Tm}\hat{Q}_m + \lambda_{Tn}\hat{Q}_n = \hat{T} - \delta_T(\hat{w} - \hat{r}) \tag{2.25}$$

where $\quad \delta_L = \lambda_{Lx}\theta_{Tx}\sigma_x + \lambda_{Lm}\theta_{Tm}\sigma_m + \lambda_{Ln}\theta_{Tn}\sigma_n$

$\quad\quad\quad \delta_T = \lambda_{Tx}\theta_{Lx}\sigma_x + \lambda_{Tm}\theta_{Lm}\sigma_m + \lambda_{Tn}\theta_{Ln}\sigma_n$

In general, δ_L is the aggregate percentage saving in labor inputs at unchanged outputs associated with a 1 percent rise in the relative wage rate, the saving resulting from the adjustment to less labor-intensive techniques in [all three] industries as relative wages rise.[7]

It will be necessary at a later stage to show that the exogenous prices of exportables and importables uniquely determine the two factor rewards, but this will only occur if both of these commodities, in addition to the nontradable good, are produced domestically. Yet there is nothing in the model to guarantee positive solutions for Q_x and Q_m. To ensure that all three commodities are in fact produced, it is sufficient that the factor-endowment ratio that is obtained after the required inputs for nontradables have been subtracted from the total available supply of each factor must lie between the factor intensities of the two tradable industries. It is *not* necessary that the factor ratio of the nontradable industry be intermediate between the factor ratios of the two traded goods.

In Figure 2-2, three unit-value isoquants (one for each commodity) are drawn tangent to the factor- price ratio, indicating that all three goods will be produced. The nontradable industry is assumed to be the least labor-intensive industry. The dotted line shows the factor-endowment ratio available for the production of the two tradables. For both to be produced, this line must lie between $(L/T)_{Q_x}$ and $(L/T)_{Q_m}$. If the line is steeper than $(L/T)_{Q_x}$, only exportables and nontradables will be produced or if it is flatter than $(L/T)_{Q_m}$ only importables and nontradables will be produced.

Demand Conditions

Income derived from the production of the three commodities is either saved or spent on consumption. Total expenditures are then apportioned among the three goods, subject to the requirement that, for the exportable commodity, output must exceed domestic demand, for the importable commodity, the reverse must be true and for the nontradable good, domestic output and consumption must be equal.

The demand conditions in the economy are given by

$$A_x = A_x(p_x, p_m, p_n, E) \qquad (2.26)$$

$$A_m = A_m(p_x, p_m, p_n, E) \qquad (2.27)$$

$$A_n = A_n(p_x, p_m, p_n, E) \qquad (2.28)$$

where A_x, A_m, and A_n are domestic demands for the exportable, importable, and nontradable, while E represents total expenditures. By definition, $A_n = Q_n$, but the link between domestic demand and output in the two tradable industries is provided by the trade balance. All three demand functions are assumed to exhibit zero-degree homogeneity with respect to all prices and total expenditures. This means that an equal proportional

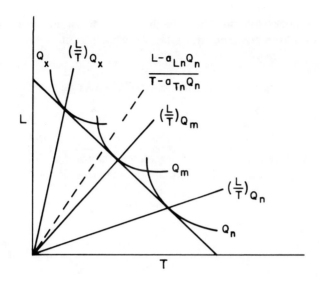

Figure 2-2. Unit-Value Isoquants of Q_x, Q_m and Q_n and Their Factor Ratios

increase in all variables results in unchanged quantities demanded. In terms of proportional changes, the demand relationships are

$$\hat{A}_x = \eta_{A_x, p_x}\, \hat{p}_x + \eta_{A_x, p_m}\, \hat{p}_m + \eta_{A_x, p_n}\, \hat{p}_n + \eta_{A_x, E}\, \hat{E} \qquad (2.29)$$

$$\hat{A}_m = \eta_{A_m, p_x}\, \hat{p}_x + \eta_{A_m, p_m}\, \hat{p}_m + \eta_{A_m, p_n}\, \hat{p}_n + \eta_{A_m, E}\, \hat{E} \qquad (2.30)$$

$$\hat{A}_n = \eta_{A_n, p_x}\, \hat{p}_x + \eta_{A_n, p_m}\, \hat{p}_m + \eta_{A_n, p_n}\, \hat{p}_n + \eta_{A_n, E}\, \hat{E} \qquad (2.31)$$

where the η's represent elasticities of the first subscripted variable with respect to the second subscripted variable (e.g., $\eta_{A_x, p_x} = (\partial A_x/\partial p_x)/(p_x/A_x)$). All three expenditure elasticities are assumed to be positive while own-price elasticities are negative and cross-price elasticities are positive.[c]

If $\hat{p}_x = \hat{p}_m = \hat{p}_n = \hat{E}$, then $\hat{A}_x = \hat{A}_m = \hat{A}_n = 0$ and $\eta_{j, p_x} + \eta_{j, p_m} + \eta_{j, p_n} + \eta_{j, E} = 0$ ($j = A_x, A_m, A_n$). There are additional constraints on the elasticities to be derived from the expenditure identity below.

Income, Expenditures, and the Trade Balance

The supply and demand sides of the model may now be linked by defining total income, total expenditures, and the trade balance. In the absence of

---

[c] All goods are substitutes for each other and none of them is an inferior good.

profits, total money income Y may be defined either in terms of returns to factors or total revenue from the sale of products. Thus

$$Y = wL + rT = p_x Q_x + p_m Q_m + p_n Q_n \qquad (2.32)$$

In terms of proportional changes, the equation becomes

$$\hat{Y} = \theta_L(\hat{w} + \hat{L}) + \theta_T(\hat{r} + \hat{T})$$
$$= \theta_x(\hat{p}_x + \hat{Q}_x) + \theta_m(\hat{p}_m + \hat{Q}_m) + \theta_n(\hat{p}_n + \hat{Q}_n) \qquad (2.33)$$

where θ_L and θ_T are the shares of labor and land in total income and θ_x, θ_m, and θ_n are the shares of the three commodities in total income. From their definitions, we know that $\theta_L + \theta_T = \theta_x + \theta_m + \theta_n = 1$.

Total expenditures on the three goods are given by

$$E = p_x A_x + p_m A_m + p_n A_n \qquad (2.34)$$

Differentiating this equation with respect to p_x, p_m, p_n (with all three prices set initially equal to one) and E provides four other constraints on the demand elasticities, namely

$$\theta_{A_x}(1 + \eta_{A_x, p_x}) + \theta_{A_m} \eta_{A_m, p_x} + \theta_{A_n} \eta_{A_n, p_x} = 0$$

$$\theta_{A_x} \eta_{A_x, p_m} + \theta_{A_m}(1 + \eta_{A_m, p_m}) + \theta_{A_n} \eta_{A_n, p_m} = 0$$

$$\theta_{A_x} \eta_{A_x, p_n} + \theta_{A_m} \eta_{A_m, p_n} + \theta_{A_n}(1 + \eta_{A_n, p_n}) = 0$$

$$\theta_{A_x} \eta_{A_x, E} + \theta_{A_m} \eta_{A_m, E} + \theta_{A_n} \eta_{A_n, E} = 1$$

where θ_{A_x}, θ_{A_m}, and θ_{A_n} represent the share of each commodity in total expenditures. Allowing for proportional changes in all variables, equation (2.34) becomes

$$\hat{E} = \theta_{A_x}(\hat{p}_x + \hat{A}_x) + \theta_{A_m}(\hat{p}_m + \hat{A}_m) + \theta_{A_n}(\hat{p}_n + \hat{A}_n) \qquad (2.35)$$

We may also derive a price index akin to a GNP deflator, which is

$$p = \theta_x p_x + \theta_m p_m + \theta_n p_n \qquad (2.36)$$

Assuming initial prices equal to unity, this equation in terms of proportional changes is

$$\hat{p} = \theta_x \hat{p}_x + \theta_m \hat{p}_m + \theta_n \hat{p}_n \qquad (2.37)$$

Finally, the trade balance represents the difference between income and expenditures. Thus

$$B = Y - E = p_x(Q_x - A_x) + p_m(Q_m - A_m) \qquad (2.38)$$

where $Q_x - A_x > 0$ and $Q_m - A_m < 0$. But trade equilibrium is maintained under all circumstances because of the assumed equality of income and expenditures. Thus $\hat{E} = \hat{Y}$. A positive trade balance, on the other hand, would imply an equivalent amount of saving in the domestic economy.[d] By way of contrast, the foreign trade balance is constrained to be zero, not because of any assumption about saving on their part, but because the rest of the world is essentially a closed economy.

One last variable needs to be explored: the exchange rate. With an adjustable-peg system of exchange rates, $\hat{\pi}$ in equations (2.20) and (2.21) is exogenous. But if the SOE allows the exchange rate to adjust to market forces, $\hat{\pi}$ becomes endogenous to the system. Without capital flows, only commodity trade determines the supply and demand conditions in the foreign exchange market. But trade equilibrium is maintained at all points in time by the zero-saving assumption and not by movements in the exchange rate. In other words, equilibrium in the foreign exchange market is consistent with any positive exchange rate and therefore $\hat{\pi}$ is indeterminate.

The system is now fully determined. Assembling all the relevant equations in one place, the complete structure of the commodity and factor markets comes into focus:

$$\lambda_{Lx}\hat{Q}_x + \lambda_{Lm}\hat{Q}_m + \lambda_{Ln}\hat{Q}_n = \hat{L} + \delta_L(\hat{w} - \hat{r}) \qquad (2.24)$$

$$\lambda_{Tx}\hat{Q}_x + \lambda_{Tm}\hat{Q}_m + \lambda_{Tn}\hat{Q}_n = \hat{T} - \delta_T(\hat{w} - \hat{r}) \qquad (2.25)$$

$$\theta_{Lx}\hat{w} + \theta_{Tx}\hat{r} = \hat{p}_x \qquad (2.17)$$

$$\theta_{Lm}\hat{w} + \theta_{Tm}\hat{r} = \hat{p}_m \qquad (2.18)$$

$$\theta_{Ln}\hat{w} + \theta_{Tn}\hat{r} = \hat{p}_n \qquad (2.19)$$

$$\hat{p}_x = \hat{p}_x^* + \hat{\pi} \qquad (2.20)$$

$$\hat{p}_m = \hat{p}_m^* + \hat{\pi} \qquad (2.21)$$

$$\hat{A}_x = \eta_{A_x, \nu_x}\hat{p}_x + \eta_{A_x, \nu_m}\hat{p}_m + \eta_{A_x, \nu_n}\hat{p}_n + \eta_{A_x, E}\hat{E} \qquad (2.29)$$

$$\hat{A}_m = \eta_{A_m, \nu_x}\hat{p}_x + \eta_{A_m, \nu_m}\hat{p}_m + \eta_{A_m, \nu_n}\hat{p}_n + \eta_{A_m, E}\hat{E} \qquad (2.30)$$

$$\hat{A}_n = \eta_{A_n, \nu_x}\hat{p}_x + \eta_{A_n, \nu_m}\hat{p}_m + \eta_{A_n, \nu_n}\hat{p}_n + \eta_{A_n, E}\hat{E} \qquad (2.31)$$

$$\hat{E} = \hat{Y} \qquad (2.39)$$

$$\hat{Y} = \theta_x(\hat{p}_x + \hat{Q}_x) + \theta_m(\hat{p}_m + \hat{Q}_m) + \theta_n(\hat{p}_n + \hat{Q}_n) \qquad (2.33)$$

$$\hat{p} = \theta_x\hat{p}_x + \theta_m\hat{p}_m + \theta_n\hat{p}_n \qquad (2.37)$$

$$\hat{A}_n = \hat{Q}_n \qquad (2.40)$$

Equations (2.17), (2.18) and (2.19) have been simplified using (2.22). This

[d]It may be more accurate to define $Y - E$ as "hoarding" since saving refers to the difference between income and consumption. In this study the two terms are treated as being synonymous.

14-equation system serves to provide solutions for the following endogenous variables: $\hat{Q}_x$, $\hat{Q}_m$, $\hat{Q}_n$, $\hat{w}$, $\hat{r}$, $\hat{p}_x$, $\hat{p}_m$, $\hat{p}_n$, $\hat{A}_x$, $\hat{A}_m$, $\hat{A}_n$, $\hat{E}$, $\hat{Y}$, and $\hat{p}$. The exogenous variables are $\hat{L}$, $\hat{T}$, $\hat{p}_x^*$ and $\hat{p}^*$. If the exchange rate is held constant, then $\hat{\pi} = 0$, but if flexible exchange rates prevail, then $\hat{\pi}$ becomes indeterminate. This indeterminacy is eliminated when both commodity and capital flows are allowed, a situation which will be examined in Chapter 3.

Some Applications of the Model

With these equations of the model, it is now possible to investigate some familiar theorems in international trade theory as well as some propositions which are only of relevance to small open economies.

Factor-Price Equalization

Under some conditions (enumerated, for instance, by H.R. Heller[8]), price equalization of traded goods results in factor prices also being equalized. If production technology for the two traded goods in the rest of the world is given by

$$\begin{bmatrix} a_{Lx}^* & a_{Lm}^* \\ a_{Tx}^* & a_{Tm}^* \end{bmatrix} = \phi \begin{bmatrix} a_{Lx} & a_{Lm} \\ a_{Tx} & a_{Tm} \end{bmatrix}$$

where ϕ is a scalar and if there are no impediments to trade, resulting in $p_x = \pi p_x^*$ and $p_m = \pi p_m^*$, then equations (2.10), (2.11), (2.13), and (2.14) can be altered to

$$a_{Lx}w + a_{Tx}r = p_x = \pi p_x^* = \pi\phi a_{Lx}w^* + \pi\phi a_{Tx}r^* \qquad (2.41)$$

$$a_{Lm}w + a_{Tm}r = p_m = \pi p_m^* = \pi\phi a_{Lm}w^* + \pi\phi a_{Tm}r^* \qquad (2.42)$$

from which we derive

$$w = \pi\phi w^* \qquad (2.43)$$

$$r = \pi\phi r^* \qquad (2.44)$$

Since the factor-price equalization theorem deals with real returns or relative factor rewards, we can divide (2.43) and (2.44) by p_x or p_m to obtain

$$\frac{w}{p_x} = \phi \frac{w^*}{p_x^*} \quad \text{or} \quad \frac{w}{p_m} = \phi \frac{w^*}{p_m^*}$$

$$\frac{r}{p_x} = \phi \frac{r^*}{p_x^*} \quad \text{or} \quad \frac{r}{p_m} = \phi \frac{r^*}{p_m^*}$$

Or we can divide (2.43) by (2.44) to derive

$$\frac{w}{r} = \frac{w^*}{r^*}$$

Nominal factor prices will be equalized in terms of each currency, as well, if $\phi = 1$. In the case of a small open economy, factor-price equalization is achieved by the home country adjusting completely to prices in the rest of the world rather than the price of the scarce factor falling and the price of the abundant factor rising in the domestic economy with the opposite occurring abroad, as would be the case in the conventional analysis.

To investigate the possibility of price equalization of the nontradable, rewrite equation (2.12) in terms of foreign factor prices as

$$a_{Ln} \pi\phi w^* + a_{Tn} \pi\phi r^* = p_n \tag{2.45}$$

In the foreign country,

$$a_{Ln}^* w^* + a_{Tn}^* r^* = p_n^* \tag{2.46}$$

If $\phi a_{Ln} = a_{Ln}^*$ and $\phi a_{Tn} = a_{Tn}^*$, then $p_n = \pi p_n^*$. That is, input requirements of the two factors must be the same except for the scalar. In other words, even though the commodity is prevented from entering trade, the domestic price will be the same as in the rest of the world as long as the production techniques are uniform.

The Exchange Rate and Relative Prices

In a standard devaluation model, the terms of trade are allowed to vary when a change in the exchange rate takes place. Normally, the terms of trade will improve after a devaluation if the product of the supply elasticities of exports and imports is less than the product of the demand elasticities.[9] For a small open economy, however, the world prices of exportables and importables are exogenous and a devaluation will increase the domestic price of both by the extent of the change in the exchange rate. Hence, the terms of trade, in both the domestic and foreign currencies, remain unchanged. The question then is: What is the effect of a devaluation on the relative price of tradables and nontradables? To examine this question, combine equations (2.17) with (2.20) and (2.18) with (2.21) and remembering the result of (2.22),

$$\theta_{Lx}\hat{w} + \theta_{Tx}\hat{r} = \hat{p}_x^* + \hat{\pi} \qquad (2.47)$$

$$\theta_{Lm}\hat{w} + \theta_{Tm}\hat{r} = \hat{p}_m^* + \hat{\pi} \qquad (2.48)$$

Since the devaluation by the home country cannot affect foreign prices, $\hat{p}_x^* = \hat{p}_m^* = 0$, and we can solve for $\hat{w}$ and $\hat{r}$.

$$\hat{w} = \frac{1}{|\theta'|} \ (\theta_{Tm} - \theta_{Tx}) \ \hat{\pi} = \hat{\pi} \qquad (2.49)$$

$$\hat{r} = \frac{1}{|\theta'|} \ (\theta_{Lx} - \theta_{Lm})\hat{\pi} = \hat{\pi} \qquad (2.50)$$

Substituting these values into (2.19),

$$\hat{p}_n = (\theta_{Ln} + \theta_{Tn}) \ \hat{\pi} = \hat{\pi} \qquad (2.51)$$

From this result it can be seen that a devaluation ($\hat{\pi} > 0$) leads to equal increases in all commodity and factor prices and thus no change in relative prices.

These conclusions about the effect of a devaluation on relative prices appear to be contrary to those of Eitan Berglas and Assaf Razin. They state, "Relative prices in a small country can change as a result of devaluation only if nontradable commodities are admitted into the model."[10] However, by itself, the introduction of nontraded goods leaves unchanged their description of the conventional approach, namely, ". . . for a small country, all commodity prices . . . are determined by the rest of the world. . . . Devaluation does not change relative commodity prices; instead it changes internal prices in terms of the home currency."[11] In fact, their analysis of the effects of a devaluation on relative prices rests on the special assumptintion that the government is able to peg the "real exchange rate" (that is, the price of tradables divided by the price of nontradables) at a disequilibrium level.

The results derived in the above equations will also hold true if the exchange rate is held constant and world prices of the two traded goods change by the same proportion. In this context, it can be seen that external inflationary pressures are transferred completely to the small open economy since the price of nontradables cannot be held constant in the face of increases in world prices of tradables. The only option available to this country is to appreciate its currency if it desires to maintain price stability.[e]

The Stolper-Samuelson Theorem

If, on the other hand, we assume that the price of only one of the traded

---

[e]This topic will be developed more fully in Chapter 6.

commodities rises, we obtain what Jones calls a magnification effect. The essence of the argument is that if the price of the labor-intensive commodity (Q_x) rises relative to that of the other traded good (Q_m), wages will rise by more than the increae in the price of Q_x and rental rates of land will fall relative to the price of Q_m. While the Stolper-Samuelson theorem deals with tariffs as the source of the change in relative commodity prices, we can achieve the same results by assuming that $\hat{p}_x^* > \hat{p}_m^* = 0$. Then

$$\hat{w} = \frac{1}{|\theta'|} (1 - \theta_{Lm})\hat{p}_x^* \tag{2.52}$$

$$\hat{r} = \frac{1}{|\theta'|} (-\theta_{Lm})\hat{p}_x^* \tag{2.53}$$

Since $(1 - \theta_{Lm}) > |\theta'|$,

$$\hat{w} > \hat{p}_x^* > \hat{p}_m^* > \hat{r}$$

which is the same result derived by Jones. The effect on the price of the nontradable commodity is determined by

$$\hat{p}_n = \frac{\theta_{Ln} - \theta_{Lm}}{\theta_{Lx} - \theta_{Lm}} \hat{p}_x^* \tag{2.54}$$

If the nontradable is less labor-intensive than than the importable good, then $\hat{p}_n < 0$. If, however, the labor intensity of Q_n is intermediate between Q_x and Q_m, the price of Q_n will rise but less than the price of Q_x. Finally, if Q_n is more labor-intensive than Q_x, its price will rise more than the price of Q_x but less than the wage rate.[12] No matter what happens to the price of nontradables, the *real* wage rate has risen. This can be seen from the following relationship:

$$\hat{w} - \hat{p} = \frac{\hat{p}_x^*}{|\theta'|} (1 - \theta_{Lx}\theta_x - \theta_{Lm}\theta_m - \theta_{Ln}\theta_n) > 0$$

since $\theta_x + \theta_m + \theta_n = 1$ and $\theta_{Lx}, \theta_{Lm}, \theta_{Ln} < 1$. By the same token, $\hat{r} - \hat{p} < 0$ and the *real* rate of return to land has fallen.

The Rybczynski Theorem

As Jones points out, the Rybczynski theorem is the dual of the Stolper-Samuelson theorem. It deals with the magnification effect on outputs of disproportionate increases in the availability of the two factors, in the face of constant terms of trade and balanced trade. We therefore assume that

$\hat{L} > \hat{T} = 0$, $\hat{Y} = \hat{E}$ and $\hat{p}_x^* = \hat{p}_m^* = 0$. From the last assumption, $\hat{w} = \hat{r} = \hat{p}_n = 0$ follows. The required equations are

$$\lambda_{Lx} \hat{Q}_x + \lambda_{Lm} \hat{Q}_m + \lambda_{Ln} \hat{Q}_n = \hat{L} \tag{2.55}$$

$$\lambda_{Tx} \hat{Q}_x + \lambda_{Tm} \hat{Q}_m + \lambda_{Tn} \hat{Q}_n = 0 \tag{2.56}$$

$$\hat{A}_n = \eta_{A_n, E} \hat{E} \tag{2.57}$$

$$\hat{E} = \hat{Y} \tag{2.58}$$

$$\hat{Y} = \theta_L \hat{L} \tag{2.59}$$

Therefore, since $\hat{A}_n = \hat{Q}_n$,

$$\hat{Q}_n = \eta_{An,E} \theta_L \hat{L}$$

Because of the growth in the labor force, money income rises, which leads to higher expenditures on all goods including nontradables, with the extent of the increase depending only on the share of labor in total income and the expenditure elasticity on nontradables. Substituting the value of $\hat{Q}_n$ into (2.55) and (2.56) we obtain

$$\hat{Q}_x = \frac{\hat{L}}{|\lambda'|} [\lambda_{Tm}(1 - \lambda_{Ln}\eta_{An,E}\theta_L) + \lambda_{Lm}\lambda_{Tn}\eta_{An,E}\theta_L] \tag{2.60}$$

$$\hat{Q}_m = -\frac{\hat{L}}{|\lambda'|} [\lambda_{Tx}(1 - \lambda_{Ln}\eta_{An,E}\theta_L) + \lambda_{Lx}\lambda_{Tn}\eta_{An,E}\theta_L] \tag{2.61}$$

Therefore, $\hat{Q}_x > 0$ and $\hat{Q}_m < 0$ if $\lambda_{Ln} \eta_{An,E} \theta_L < 1$. This is the same generalization of the Rybczynski theorem for the three-commodity case developed by Komiya,[13] but only part of the magnification effect can be proven, namely that $\hat{L} > \hat{T} > \hat{Q}_m$. Moreover, there is nothing in the model to constrain the expenditure elasticity to a value small enough so that the above-stated condition holds. Therefore, rewriting equations (2.60) and (2.61) produces

$$\hat{Q}_x = \frac{\hat{L}}{|\lambda'|} [\lambda_{Tm} + \eta_{An,E} \theta_L(\lambda_{Lm}\lambda_{Tn} - \lambda_{Tm}\lambda_{Ln})] \tag{2.60'}$$

$$\hat{Q}_m = -\frac{\hat{L}}{|\lambda'|} [\lambda_{Tx} + \eta_{An,E} \theta_L(\lambda_{Lx} \lambda_{Tn} - \lambda_{Tx}\lambda_{Ln})] \tag{2.61'}$$

The expression in the parentheses in (2.60') is positive if the importable is more labor-intensive than the nontradable, while in (2.61'), the expression in the parentheses is positive if the exportable is more labor-intensive than the nontradable.

Given that the exportable is assumed to be more labor-intensive than the importable (that is, $|\lambda'| > 0$), there are three possible orderings of labor intensity for the three goods. For each ordering, the effect of an increase in the labor supply on the outputs of the three goods is shown in Table 2-1.

As can be seen from this table, only in case (3) does the Rybczynski theorem hold. In the other two cases, some of the ambiguity is eliminated if $\eta_{A_n, E} \, \theta_L > 1$. In that event, $\hat{Q}_n > \hat{L}$ and the two tradable industries will have less labor available to them than before, requiring some contraction of output.

The Effect of Taxes and Subsidies on Relative Prices

It has been shown that a domestic tariff on the importable increases its price in the home country while a foreign tariff on the exportable lowers its domestic price. Now, consider the effects of domestic taxes or subsidies on the two tradable commodities as well as on nontradables. Since taxes and subsidies are symmetrical, it is possible to focus on the latter to conform to Jones's analysis.[14] In his terminology, p_j is the market price of commodity j ($j = x, m, n$), but the producer receives $s_j p_j$ where s_j is equal to one plus the *ad valorem* rate of subsidy.[f]

First, consider a subsidy to the producers of nontradables. Equation (2.19) becomes

$$\theta_{Ln} \, \hat{w} + \theta_{Tn} \, \hat{r} = \hat{p}_n + \hat{s}_n \tag{2.62}$$

Since $\hat{p}_x = \hat{p}_m = 0$, therefore $\hat{w} = \hat{r} = 0$ and hence $\hat{p}_n = -\hat{s}_n$. In other words, the market price of the nontradable falls by the amount of the subsidy. The relative price of tradables to nontradables now rises causing consumers to readjust their consumption bundle, increasing their demand for nontradables at the expense of tradables. Income will remain constant since $\hat{w} = \hat{r} = \hat{L} = \hat{T} = 0$ and if balanced trade is maintained, $\hat{E} = 0$. Thus

$$\hat{A}_n = -\eta_{A_n, \, p_n} \, \hat{s}_n > 0$$

The output of nontradables must also rise to meet the higher demand for this commodity. Changes in the outputs of the other two commodities are given by

$$\hat{Q}_x = \frac{\eta_{A_n, \, p_n} \hat{s}_n}{|\lambda'|} \, [\lambda_{Tm}\lambda_{Ln} - \lambda_{Lm}\lambda_{Tn}] \tag{2.63}$$

$$\hat{Q}_m = \frac{\eta_{A_n, \, p_n} \hat{s}_n}{|\lambda'|} \, [\lambda_{Lx}\lambda_{Tn} - \lambda_{Tx}\lambda_{Ln}] \tag{2.64}$$

---

[f]In the case of a tax, $s_j = 1/(1 + t_j)$ where t_j is the *ad valorem* rate of tax.

Table 2-1
Changes in Output of Exportables, Importables, and Nontradables as a Result of an Increase in the Supply of Labor

	Orderings of Labor Intensity		
	(1)	*(2)*	*(3)*
Commodity	$Q_x > Q_n > Q_m$	$Q_n > Q_x > Q_m$	$Q_x > Q_m > Q_n$
$\hat{Q}_x$	?	?	(+)
$\hat{Q}_m$	(−)	?	(−)
$\hat{Q}_n$	(+)	(+)	(+)

Note: For brevity, Q_x represents $(L/T)_{Q_x}$, etc.

Table 2-2
The Effect of a Subsidy to Nontradables on the Outputs of Exportables and Importables

	Orderings of Labor Intensity		
	(1)	*(2)*	*(3)*
Commodity	$Q_x > Q_n > Q_m$	$Q_n > Q_x > Q_m$	$Q_x > Q_m > Q_n$
$\hat{Q}_x$	(−)	(−)	(+)
$\hat{Q}_m$	(−)	(+)	(−)

The direction of change for Q_x and Q_m is not clear unless the labor intensity of the three goods is ordered. (This is the same problem as that encountered with the Rybczynski theorem.) In Table 2-2, the effect on the output of exportables and importables under the three ordering assumptions is shown. With an increase in the output of nontradables and in the absence of increases in factor availability, there must be some contraction in one or both tradable industries, a condition which is satisfied by all three intensity orderings.

If a subsidy is applied to the exportable, producers will receive for each unit $s_x p_x$ or $\pi p_x^*[1/(1 + \tau_x^*)]s_x$. Combining equations (2.17) and (2.20) with $\hat{\pi} = 0$ and introducing the subsidy, produces

$$\theta_{Lx}\,\hat{w} + \theta_{Tx}\,\hat{r} = \hat{p}_x^* + \hat{s}_x \qquad (2.65)$$

But a subsidy can have no influence on the foreign price of exportables and therefore $\hat{p}_x^* = 0$. Thus the subsidy has the same effect as that generated by an exogenous change in p_x^*, a situation which has been analyzed in the discussion of the Stolper-Samuelson theorem.

Lastly, a subsidy to the importable industry yields a per-unit revenue of

$s_m p_m$ or $\pi p_m^*(1 + \tau_m)s_m$. The factor-commodity price relationship in this industry now becomes

$$\theta_{Lm}\,\hat{w} + \theta_{Tm}\,\hat{r} = \hat{p}_m^* + \hat{s}_m \qquad (2.66)$$

which is symmetrical to the subsidy on the exportable.

In conclusion, a subsidy to the nontradable industry causes a proportional forward shifting of the benefits to the consumers, while subsidies to either of the tradable industries are shifted backward, affecting factor rewards in a magnified fashion.

Optimal Tariffs and Taxes

Earlier discussion dealt with the existence of tariffs as a means of delineating traded and nontraded goods and the effect of various taxes or subsidies on relative prices. It is now convenient to determine the optimum levels of all types of taxes: foreign trade taxes, domestic commodity taxes, and taxes on factors of production. Since Jones's model does not lend itself to a constrained optimization procedure, a different model based on that of R.W. Boadway, Shlomo Maital and M.F.J. Prachowny[15] will be employed.

As a general proposition, it has already been proven[16] that if a country such as an SOE is unable to influence its terms of trade, it should follow a free trade policy. Under these circumstances, the problem becomes one of determining whether these conclusions are altered when nontraded commodities and the possibility of domestic taxes are introduced into the analysis.

Assume a utility function of the form

$$U = U(A_x, A_m, A_n, L) \qquad (2.67)$$

Not only does the domestic consumption of the three commodities enter the utility function, but so does L, since it is the obverse of a fourth good, leisure. This utility function has two constraints: the trade balance and the production possibilities function. The trade balance, defined in terms of foreign prices, is

$$p_x^*(Q_x - A_x) - p_m^*(A_m - Q_m) = 0 \qquad (2.68)$$

The transformation function is

$$\Gamma(Q_x, Q_m, Q_n, L) = 0 \qquad (2.69)$$

which is assumed to exhibit constant returns to scale. For purposes of simplicity, only one factor, L, is assumed to exist.

The presence of domestic and foreign trade taxes implies three sets of prices: foreign prices p^*, domestic producer prices p, and domestic consumer prices q, related by the following definitions:

$$p_x = p_x^*(1 - \tau_x)$$
$$p_m = p_m^*(1 + \tau_m)$$
$$q_j = p_j(1 - t_j), \quad (j = x, m, n)$$
$$w' = w(1 + t_L)$$

$$(2.70)$$

where τ_x is the *ad valorem* rate of tax on exports, τ_m is the *ad valorem* tariff on imports, t_j is the rate of tax on domestic consumption of the three commodities, t_L is the rate of tax on the producer price of labor, w', and w is the net wage.

Since we are interested only in the distortionary effects of these various taxes rather than their revenue-generating effects, I assume lump-sum redistribution payments. The constrained maximization problem involves the following Lagrangian expression:

$$H = U(A_x, A_m, A_n, L) + \psi[p_x^*(Q_x - A_x) - p_m^*(A_m - Q_m)]$$
$$- \chi[F(Q_x, Q_m, Q_n, L)] \qquad (2.71)$$

The control variables in this problem are Q_x, Q_m, Q_n, L, A_x, and A_m. Differentiating with respect to these variables provides the following first-order conditions:

$$\frac{\partial H}{\partial Q_x} = \psi p_x^* - \chi \frac{\partial F}{\partial Q_x} = 0$$

$$\frac{\partial H}{\partial Q_m} = \psi p_m^* - \chi \frac{\partial F}{\partial Q_m} = 0$$

$$\frac{\partial H}{\partial Q_n} = \frac{\partial U}{\partial A_n} - \chi \frac{\partial F}{\partial Q_n} = 0$$

$$\frac{\partial H}{\partial L} = \frac{\partial U}{\partial L} - \chi \frac{\partial F}{\partial L} = 0$$

$$\frac{\partial H}{\partial A_x} = \frac{\partial U}{\partial A_x} - \psi p_x^* = 0$$

$$\frac{\partial H}{\partial A_m} = \frac{\partial U}{\partial A_m} - \psi p_m^* = 0$$

$$(2.72)$$

Choosing a unit of account such that the marginal utility of income is unity, the following definitions are derived:

$$p_x = \chi \partial F/\partial Q_x \qquad\qquad q_x = \partial U/\partial A_x$$
$$p_m = \chi \partial F/\partial Q_m \qquad\qquad q_m = \partial U/\partial A_m$$
$$p_n = \chi \partial F/\partial Q_n \qquad\qquad q_n = \partial U/\partial A_n$$
$$w' = -\chi \partial F/\partial L \qquad\qquad w = -\partial U/\partial L$$

Also, since ψ is the product of the shadow price of foreign exchange and the actual exchange rate, we can set $\psi = 1$ by an appropriate choice of the exchange rate. Substituting these definitions into equations (2.72), we obtain the following optimal tax rules:

$$p_x^* = p_x$$
$$p_m^* = p_m$$
$$q_n = p_n$$
$$w = w'$$
$$q_x = p_x^*$$
$$q_m = p_m^*$$

These rules require that

$$\tau_x = \tau_m = t_x = t_m = t_n = t_L = 0$$

Thus a small open economy should not introduce any distortions by way of domestic or foreign trade taxes. In the absence of revenue needs, the government in this economy has no role to play; it should collect no taxes and make no redistribution payments. If, however, the government provides a public good for which it then requires tax revenue and if these taxes cannot be levied in lump-sum form, then distortionary *domestic* taxes should be imposed in order to reach a second-best optimum. It should not, even under these circumstances, impose trade taxes. Only if domestic taxes are infeasible should the small open economy levy foreign trade taxes to provide the necessary government revenue.[17]

While an SOE would not find it in its own best interests to impose any trade taxes if all countries started from a position of free trade, how should it react to a foreign tariff on its exportable commodity? In the more standard case of two large countries, both with an ability to influence the terms of trade, H.G. Johnson[18] has shown that retaliation is possible and may even be beneficial for one of the countries. Here, imposing a retaliatory tariff has two desirable effects: (1) it improves the terms of trade for the home country compared to the preretaliation situation; and (2) it provides bargaining power for the retaliating country in any negotiations to reduce or remove tariffs. For an SOE, however, no benefits can be garnered from

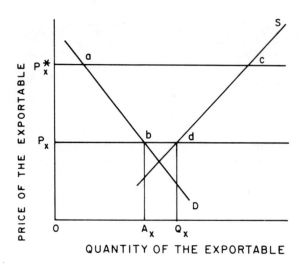

Figure 2-3. The Exportable Commodity Market Facing a Foreign Tariff

either source. Any foreign tariff causes the small country to be below its welfare maximum. The size and source of this welfare loss can be shown in a partial-equilibrium setting of the exportable market in Figure 2-3.

In this diagram, p_x^* is given by foreign demand and supply conditions. The domestic price, p_x, will be lower by the amount $1/(1 + \tau_x^*)$. At this price, domestic consumption is OA_x while output is OQ_x. If the world price (p_x^*) prevailed, there would be a reduction in consumer surplus of $p_x^* p_x ba$; at the same time, producer surplus would rise by $p_x^* p_x dc$. Thus the foreign tariff causes a net loss equal to $abdc$. The SOE cannot alleviate the situation by an export tax since that would raise the price of the exportable in the foreign country above p_x^*, resulting in a complete loss of the foreign market. It could impose a domestic tax on the exportable to consumers and a subsidy to producers, but this would merely redistribute income within the economy without a gain in welfare for the economy as a whole, unless we were prepared to assign weights to various individuals in a social welfare function.

The crux of the problem for a small open economy can be seen by an appeal to the analysis of J.N. Bhagwati and V.K. Ramaswami.[19]

The source of the distortion is the discrepancy between the foreign and domestic marginal rates of transformation. The normal correction for this is a trade tax rather than a domestic tax-cum-subsidy scheme. But the SOE takes as given the foreign marginal rate of transformation and the foreign tariff, both of which determine the terms of trade, leaving no opportunity for the SOE to redress the situation with a tariff or export tax. Levying such trade taxes is also not beneficial from the point of view of providing bargaining power in tariff negotiations since the SOE's share in world trade is so small that it is unlikely to have any strength in such negotiations.

Summary

In this chapter, the commodity and factor markets of a small open economy have been portrayed in a well-behaved and self-contained model based on the Heckscher-Ohlin theory of factor proportions.[g] While many of the standard theorems in international trade theory require some additional assumptions compared with the traditional model, no serious problems are presented by the special characteristics of the tradable sector or the introduction of the nontradable sector. In some ways, the structure of the model is greatly simplified since events in the rest of the world may be treated as exogenous. Instead of dealing with the complex interdependence among countries in a world economy, it is possible to focus only on the SOE, which is completely dependent on the environment external to its jurisdiction.

Notes

1. M.C. Kemp, *The Pure Theory of International Trade and Investment,* Englewood Cliffs, N.J., Prentice-Hall, 1969, p. 134.

2. Ibid. The disparities in preferences or per capita income are presumably related to Burenstam Linder's theory of international trade. See S. Burenstam Linder, *An Essay on Trade and Transformation,* Uppsala, Almqvist and Wiksell, 1961.

3. Kemp, *The Pure Theory,* p. 134.

4. R.W. Jones, "The Structure of Simple General Equilibrium Models," *Journal of Political Economy* 73 (1965): 557-72.

5. Ryutaro Komiya, "Non-Traded Goods and the Pure Theory of International Trade," *International Economic Review* 8 (1967): 132-52.

6. Jones, "The Structure of Simple General Equilibrium Models," p. 560.

7. Ibid., p. 561.

---

[g]Recent empirical work on the determinants of trade patterns has failed to verify the *simple* two-factor Heckscher-Ohlin model.[20] Yet the structure of trade between the SOE and the rest of the world in this study is precisely of this form. Since the tradables produced in the SOE are identical with those produced abroad, trade based on product differentiation, technology or innovation gaps, and product life-cycles cannot be admitted into the analysis.

8. H.R. Heller, *International Trade: Theory and Empirical Evidence,* Second Edition, Englewood Cliffs, N.J., Prentice-Hall, 1973, p. 125.

9. For a proof of this proposition, see R.M. Stern, *The Balance of Payments: Theory and Economic Policy,* Chicago, Aldine Publishing Company, 1973, pp. 67-69.

10. Eitan Berglas and Assaf Razin, "Real Exchange Rate and Devaluation," *Journal of International Economics* 3 (1973): 180.

11. Ibid.

12. These results may be compared with those of Komiya, "Non-Traded Goods," p. 136.

13. Ibid., p. 141.

14. Jones, "The Structure of Simple General Equilibrium Models," p. 562.

15. R.W. Boadway, Shlomo Maital and M.F.J. Prachowny, "Optimal Tariffs, Optimal Taxes and Public Goods," *Journal of Public Economics* 2 (1973): 391-403.

16. See, for example, Heller, *International Trade,* p. 172.

17. These conclusions are based on the analysis in R.W. Boadway, Shlomo Maital and M.F.J. Prachowny, "Optimal Tariffs," which develops a simple general equilibrium model of an open economy (but not necessarily small) with an endogenously determined level of public goods provided from resources appropriated by tariff and domestic tax revenue.

18. H.G. Johnson, "Optimum Tariffs and Retaliation," *Review of Economic Studies* 21 (1953-54): 142-53.

19. J.N. Bhagwati and V.K. Ramaswami, "Domestic Distortions, Tariffs and the Theory of Optimum Subsidy," *Journal of Political Economy* 79 (1963): 44-50.

20. See, for example, R.E. Baldwin, "Determinants of the Commodity Structure of U.S. Trade," *American Economic Review* 61 (1971): 126-46.

3 The Asset Markets

Introduction

Although the small country assumption has served as a useful simplification in a number of models in international economics, its explicit incorporation into the asset markets of a policy model developed by R. A. Mundell[1] has had a powerful effect on clarifying the issue of stabilization-policy effectiveness for SOEs. In essence, his model provides an elegant proof of the proposition that fiscal policy is only operative as a stabilization instrument when fixed exchange rates prevail while monetary policy, in the form of open-market operations, is effective only under flexible exchange rates. While the analysis has been modified by Victor Argy and M. G. Porter,[2] T. F. Dernburg,[3] M. F. J. Prachowny,[4] Akira Takayama[5] and others, the conclusions derived by Mundell based on his set of assumptions have not been controverted.

In this chapter, I propose to investigate in some detail the characteristics of the asset markets in a small open economy. The assets to be considered are money and bonds, both being issued by the domestic authorities. Domestic and foreign bonds will be assumed to be perfect substitutes for each other by all investors. At a later stage, domestic equities will be introduced to allow a comparison with the results of monetary policy in a closed economy as derived by James Tobin.[6]

The framework of the analysis is a portfolio optimization model subject to a wealth constraint. Investors are assumed to apportion a given level of wealth among the various assets so as to maximize a utility function that has expected rates of return and risk as arguments. The theoretical foundations of this type of model and its limitations have already been explored in the literature based originally on H. M. Markowitz[7] and James Tobin[8] and will not be treated here.[9]

Unlike the commodity markets discussed in Chapter 2 that involved flow equilibria, the asset markets are investigated in terms of stock equilibria. This involves a dichotomization of the two sets of markets: the commodity market equilibria are subject to an income (flow) constraint while the asset market equilibria are subject to a wealth (stock) constraint. In Tobin's words: "The key behavioral assumption of this procedure is that spending decisions and portfolio decisions are independent—specifically that decisions about the accumulation of wealth are separable from decisions about its allocation.''[10] However, later when we have cause to introduce the concept of *desired* wealth, the two constraints must be interwoven and the dichotomization will disappear.

In order to provide a fairly simple first approximation of asset market behavior, both the exchange rate and the price level, as well as expectations about their future levels, will be held constant. These simplifying assumptions will be relaxed in subsequent sections in order to provide a more realistic setting for the policy models to follow in the next chapter.

Perfect Capital Mobility and the Exogeneity of the Domestic Interest Rate

Before proceeding with the analysis of the asset markets, it is necessary to investigate the assumption of perfect capital mobility that was crucial in R. A. Mundell's model. He was aware of the extreme nature of this proposition and stated, ''This assumption will overstate the case, but it has the merit of posing a stereotype toward which international financial relations seem to be heading.''[11] To provide some empirical justification, he goes on to argue that ''the assumption is not far from the truth in those financial centres of which Zurich, Amsterdam, and Brussels may be taken as examples, where the authorities already recognize their lessening ability to dominate money market conditions and insulate them from foreign influences. It should also have a high degree of relevance to a country like Canada whose financial markets are dominated to a great degree by the vast New York market.''[12] Also, R. E. Caves and G. L. Reuber voice the fear that: ''Because of the threat of massive short-term capital inflows, Canada would be unable to raise her domestic interest rate in order to restrain inflation.''[13]

Perfect capital mobility is derived from the proposition that securities (that is, bonds), whether issued at home or abroad, are considered to be perfect substitutes by all investors. In that case, both types of bonds can be aggregated into a single homogenous asset and their prices (or their yields) will be equalized throughout the world much as the prices of traded goods find a common level in all world markets if impediments to their movement are absent. To continue the analogy with tradable goods, a small open economy faces an infinitely elastic excess demand for its bonds at the going price of bonds and, therefore, it is forced to treat their price as an exogenous variable. To put it another way, the SOE provides a porportion of the total world supply of bonds but that proportion is so small that it acts as a price-taker in that market. The SOE, therefore, is an atomistic competitor not only in some commodity markets but also in one important asset market.

If supply or demand conditions for securities in the rest of the world are altered, the world interest rate will adjust accordingly and the domestic interest rate will have to follow suit so that, in the new equilibrium, domestic and foreign bonds will again be indistinguishable. Even if there are impediments to the movement of securities from one country to another (e.g., taxes on foreign bonds such as the Interest Equalization Tax imposed in the United States in 1963), interest rates will diverge, but as long as these impediments are not prohibitive and remain constant, a given proportional change in the world interest rate caused by exogenous shocks in the world market for securities will lead to an equal proportional change in the domestic interest rate. For simplicity, I will assume no impediments to the free flow of securities and under these conditions it is not inappropriate to use the world interest rate as opposed to the (identical) domestic interest rate in the domestic demand functions for various assets.

This proposition does not present any analytical difficulties as long as the exchange rate is fixed and assumed to remain constant by all investors. As outlined above, I intend to proceed on the basis of this assumption until later in the chapter, but it is worth noting at this point the interpretation attached to perfect capital mobility when exchange rates are no longer considered constant. Now, in order to avoid the risks of exchange-rate fluctuations, investors will compare the hedged yield on foreign securities against the rate of return on their own securities. Therefore, equilibrium in all securities markets requires that the unhedged interest differential between domestic and foreign bonds be equal to the premium in the forward market. Under these circumstances, the domestic interest rate is no longer completely exogenous to the asset markets of the small open economy. These considerations will receive detailed attention in this chapter's section, "The Forward Market and Flexible Exchange Rates."

The Money Market

The first asset to occupy our attention is the domestic medium of exchange—money. The most important characteristic of the money market in a small open economy is that the financial agent of the government (e.g., the central bank, the Treasury) is unable to sterilize balance-of-payments effects on the money supply. This crucial proposition will be proven after the equilibrium conditions in all asset markets have been specified, but it is necessary to take account of its possible existence in formulating the determinants of the money supply.

The Supply of Money

In considering the determinants of the money supply, conventional theory focuses on three decision-makers: the central bank, the commercial banks, and the public. In essence, the central bank determines the level of reserves (or high powered money); the commercial banks determine excess reserves; and the public determines the form in which money is held (e.g., currency, demand or time deposits).

Although important for some purposes, these interrelated decisions will not be treated here and I will focus only on the decisions of the central bank. By combining the commercial banks and the public into one entity, all money becomes "outside" money and the availability of reserves alone determines the supply of money.[a] Before proceeding with a discussion of the relationship between the central bank and the private sector, however, it is necessary to outline the asset and liability positions of the four major institutions in the system: the government, the central bank, commercial banks, and the public.

All irrelevant assets and liabilities (such as currency) as well as net worth of all institutions have been omitted in Table 3-1. The public can be construed to represent both domestic residents as well as foreigners, although the latter are assumed to hold only domestic government securities. To simplify the system, it is assumed that the total of government deposits at both the central bank and the commercial banks as well as government securities outstanding remain unchanged, implying a balanced budget. Also we combine commercial banks and the public which cancels out a number of assets and liabilities. Thus, Table 3-2 depicts the relationship between the central bank and the private sector.

The net wealth of the private sector is equal to its assets minus its liabilities. Since the private sector holds its net worth in either government securities or money, the *net* amount of money available to the private sector is equal to its deposits at the central bank minus the deposits of the government at the commercial banks.[b] This money supply is potentially alterable by three types of transactions: (1) open-market operations; (2) central bank intervention in the foreign exchange market in order to maintain the fixity of the exchange rate; and (3) shifting of government deposits between the central bank and the commercial banks. Using 100 units of the domestic currency as the basis for each of these transactions, these operations and their effect on the money supply are shown in Tables 3-3, 3-4 and 3-5.

The central bank purchases the bonds from the private sector and credits the proceeds to its deposit account. This causes an equivalent expansion of the money supply. This is shown in Table 3-3.

---

[a]Outside money, in this context, is an asset of the private sector and a liability of the government. Inside money is both an asset and a liability of the private sector.

[b]If the reader prefers to think of money as the actual medium of exchange, this can be done if reserve requirements are assumed to be 100 percent.

Table 3-1

Assets and Liabilities of the Government, the Central Bank, the Commercial Banks, and the Public

Government		Central Bank	
Deposits at the central bank	Government bonds outstanding	Government securities	Deposits of the commercial banks
Deposits at the commercial banks		International reserves	Deposits of the government

Commercial Banks		Public	
Reserves at the central bank	Deposits held by the public	Government securities	Loans from the commercial banks
Government securities	Deposits held by the government	Deposits at the commercial banks	
Loans to the public			

Table 3-2

Assets and Liabilities of the Central Bank and the Private Sector

Central Bank		Private Sector	
Government securities	Deposits of the private sector	Government securities	Deposits of the government
International reserves	Deposits of the government	Deposits at the central bank	

Table 3-3

The Effect of Expansionary Open-Market Operations

Central Bank		Private Sector	
Government securities +100	Deposits of the private sector +100	Government securities −100	
		Deposits at the central bank +100	

A balance-of-payments surplus implies that the private sector has accumulated undesired foreign exchange. Not wishing to hold this foreign currency, it sells it to the central bank at the fixed price, again receiving a

Table 3-4
The Effect of a Balance-of-Payments Surplus

Central Bank		Private Sector
International reserves $+100$	Deposits of the private sector $+100$	Deposits at the central bank $+100$
		Foreign exchange -100

Table 3-5
The Effect of Shifting Government Deposits from the Central Bank to the Private Sector

Central Bank		Private Sector	
	Deposits of the private sector $+100$	Deposits at the central bank $+100$	Deposits of the government $+100$
	Deposits of the government -100		

credit to its deposit account at the central bank, resulting in an equal increase in the money supply. If the central bank considers this expansionary effect on the money supply undesirable, it can engage in sterilization operations, which in this case involves open-market sales of securities equal to the increase in its holdings of international reserves. The resulting decline in the money supply offsets the initial increase caused by the surplus in the balance of payments. However, the central bank will now hold more international reserves and fewer government securities. It can now be seen that the success of sterilization operations depends on the existing stocks of international reserves or government securities held by the central bank. If the central bank no longer has any government securities at its disposal, it cannot sterilize a surplus;[c] if it has run out of international reserves, it cannot sterilize a deficit. For a small open economy where perfect capital mobility is assumed to exist, we will see that sterilization operations imply the immediate exhaustion of one of these assets and therefore they become infeasible.

If the central bank, on its own initiative or at the behest of the government, shifts government deposits from itself to the private sector (that is, to the commercial banks), it increases the deposits of the private sector at the central bank and the deposits of the government at the commercial banks

[c]Normally, it is unlikely that the central bank will deplete its stock of government securities, but since the government is assumed to have a balanced budget, it cannot obtain more bonds from this source.

Table 3-6
Simplified Structure of Assets and Liabilities of the Central Bank and the Private Sector

Central Bank		Private Sector	
Government securities	Deposits of the private sector	Government securities	Net wealth
International reserves		Deposits at the central bank	

equally, leaving unchanged the net supply of money available to the public. Therefore, shifting of government deposits cannot be used as a measure to change the money supply, but merely to alter its composition. Under these circumstances, the location of government deposits is irrelevant and they will be dropped from the analysis. With this simplification, the assets and liabilities of the central bank and the private sector are depicted in Table 3-6.

The central bank has assets equal to its liabilities as specified, while the net wealth of the private sector is equal to its assets. The economy as a whole has no net wealth since the assets of the private sector plus the central bank are offset by the liabilities of the government. In this system, the money supply is determined by

$$Z = S + R \tag{3.1}$$

where Z is equal to the money supply (identical to deposits of the private sector at the central bank), S defines the stock of government securities held by the central bank, and R represents the stock of international reserves.

It is important to note that R must represent the stock of *earned* reserves, or in other words, the algebraic sum of all past deficits and surpluses in the balance of payments. Depending on accounting conventions, it is possible for a central bank to accumulate international reserves without having intervened in the foreign exchange market in order to maintain the fixed exchange rate. An example would be a new allocation of Special Drawing Rights. Since such an allocation would not involve the central bank in a transaction with the commercial banks or the public, it must be omitted from the analysis. I will also assume that in the balance sheet of the central bank, international reserves have been converted into the domestic currency so that changes in the exchange rate cannot be construed as changes in the money supply.[d]

---

[d]If the SOE devalued its currency, the central bank would experience a capital gain on its holdings of international reserves, requiring bookkeeping adjustments, but a devaluation does not increase the money supply because it does not involve a transaction between the central bank and the public.

In terms of proportional changes in the variables, equation (3.1) becomes

$$\hat{Z} = \lambda_{SZ}\hat{S} + \lambda_{RZ}\hat{R} \tag{3.2}$$

where $\hat{Z} = dZ/Z$, etc. and λ_{SZ} and λ_{RZ} represent the ratio of S and R to Z, respectively. For any given proportional change in reserves through balance-of-payments disequilibrium, the open-market operations required to sterilize this effect on the money supply is

$$\hat{S} = - \frac{R}{S} \hat{R} \tag{3.3}$$

As can be seen from this equation, the necessary change in the holdings of government securities depends not only on the size of the change in reserves, but also on the initial levels of the two assets held by the central bank.

The Demand for Money

Private individuals in the economy are assumed to apportion thei. wealth between money and bonds. The proportion held in the form of money depends on the level of income normalized by the size of wealth and the interest rate on bonds. An increase in income with wealth held constant is taken to be an increase in the requirement for transactions balances, forcing individuals to hold a larger proportion of their wealth in the form of money. But an equi-proportional increase in income and wealth, leaves unaffected the ratio of money to wealth.[14] The interest rate, on the other hand, enters the demand for money function on the basis of the traditional argument of liquidity preference. In this case, however, because of perfect capital mobility and the smallness of the domestic economy, it is the world interest rate that enters the demand function since the domestic interest rate cannot deviate from the world interest rate in equilibrium. The equation summarizing these arguments can be written as

$$Z = f(Y/W, r^*) \ W \tag{3.4}$$

where Y represents both real and nominal income since the price level is held constant; r^* is the world interest rate;[e] and W is the net stock of

[e]In Chapter 2, the variable r denoted the rate of return to land, while in this chapter, the same variable represents the rate of interest on bonds. There is no simple relationship between these two variables; yet in order to economize on notation, r stands for both of these, each in its appropriate context. A closer relationship could have been established at the cost of a much more complex model. In Chapter 2, capital could have been the second factor of production, instead of land, but its supply would no longer be exogenous.[15] Then in the asset markets of this chapter, the valuation of the capital stock as expressed in equities could be substituted for the value of bonds in the analysis, leading to a direct link between the rate of return on capital

domestic wealth. Z is now interpreted as the demand for money balances. Again, since prices are held constant, it is irrelevant whether Z represents the nominal or the real stock of money. Later in the analysis when prices are allowed to change, equation (3.4) will have to be modified.

This equation indicates that the demand for money is not homogeneous of degree one with respect to wealth. On the one hand, an increase in wealth relaxes the constraint on portfolios and allows individuals to hold more of both assets, but, on the other hand, that same increase in wealth reduces the transactions demand for money. The net effect is not clear unless certain restrictions are imposed on the parameters in the equation. In terms of proportional changes, equation (3.4) is written as

$$\hat{Z} = \eta_{f,\,Y/W}\hat{Y} + \eta_{f,\,r^*}\hat{r}^* + (1 - \eta_{f,\,Y/W})\hat{W} \qquad (3.5)$$

where $\eta_{f,\,Y/W}$ represents the elasticity of Z/W with respect to Y/W, etc. In order to ensure that an increase in wealth leads to larger money holdings, it is necessary to assume that $\eta_{f,\,Y/W} < 1$.

Equilibrium in the Money Market

In equilibrium, the proportional change in the supply of money must equal the proportional change in the demand for money, allowing us to combine equations (3.2) and (3.5).

$$\lambda_{SZ}\hat{S} + \lambda_{RZ}\hat{R} = \eta_{f,\,Y/W}\hat{Y} + \eta_{f,\,r^*}\hat{r}^* + (1 - \eta_{f,\,Y/W})\hat{W} \qquad (3.6)$$

Assuming for the moment that $\hat{S} = \hat{R} = \hat{W} = 0$, this equation relates to the slope of the traditional *LM* curve in that

$$\frac{dY}{dr^*} = -\frac{Y}{r^*}\frac{\eta_{f,\,r^*}}{\eta_{f,\,Y/W}} > 0 \qquad (3.7)$$

Nevertheless, it is worth noting once more that $\hat{r}^*$ is exogenous to the domestic asset markets and in the absence of shifts in the supply or demand curves of world bonds, $\hat{r}^* = 0$ and the *LM* curve is vertical. What may be even more important is that a change in r^* will affect W (as will be shown below), in which case, equation (3.7) refers to the slope of a "wealth-compensated" *LM* curve.

The Bond Market

It was earlier assumed that all investors consider domestic and foreign

and the rate of return on equities. (The role of equities in a portfolio model is briefly discussed in the section, "Equities as a Third Asset.") But since open-market operations involve transactions in government debt, bonds cannot simply be omitted from the model.

bonds to be perfect substitutes. However, it is sufficient to specify that although domestic residents do not hold foreign bonds, foreigners are prepared to hold any excess supply of domestic bonds at the existing world interest rate. This assumption has a special advantage. If a depreciation of the domestic currency takes place (a situation to be considered later), the nominal value of domestic wealth will remain unaltered. On the other hand, foreign wealth will decrease as a result of the depreciation because of the capital loss on any holdings of domestic bonds. But since the rest of the world is large, foreign holdings of domestic bonds will be a small proportion of total foreign wealth and any change in the value of this component can be considered inconsequential. Also, given this assumption, we can focus on the supply of and demand for domestic bonds only, the stock of foreign bonds and the demand for them coming into play indirectly through their determination of the world interest rate.

The Supply of Bonds

For the time being, the government is assumed to be the only source of interest-earning assets in the economy. This total supply of bonds represents the algebraic sum of all past deficits and surpluses to the extent that deficits were financed by bond issues (as opposed to printing money) and that surpluses were used to buy back outstanding bonds (as opposed to increased money balances). But these surpluses and deficits are assumed to be a thing of the past and total bonds outstanding are therefore constant.

The supply of bonds available to the public (both domestic residents and foreigners) is equal to the total number of bonds outstanding minus those bonds held by the central bank. However, the *value* of the bonds available to the public depends on the number of bonds and their price, the latter in turn depending on the market rate of interest compared with the coupon rate and the length of time to maturity. With respect to the last factor, two extreme assumptions are possible. A bond can be either a consol or an infinitely short-term bond. In both cases, a bond represents an obligation on the part of the government to pay interest at the rate r^α per unit of time, where r is the market rate of interest and α is a parameter. If $\alpha = 0$, the bond is a consol, and if $\alpha = 1$, the bond is infinitely short-term. The present value of either bond and hence its price is

$$P_v = \int_0^\infty r^\alpha e^{-rt} = r^{\alpha-1} \begin{cases} = 1/r & \text{if } \alpha = 0 \\ = 1 & \text{if } \alpha = 1 \end{cases} \qquad (3.8)^f$$

---

[f]This method of showing the effect of maturity on the price of a bond has been brought to my attention by Alan Deardorff.

For our purposes, the consol is analytically superior since it allows for the possibility of capital gains or losses when the interest rate changes, a necessary condition for investors to hold both money and bonds. (This topic is covered in more detail in this chapter's section, "The Substitutability of Assets.")

The value of bonds held by the public is defined as

$$V = P_v v = \frac{1}{r^*} v \qquad (3.9)$$

where v represents the number of bonds available to the public. Taking proportional changes of equation (3.9) results in

$$\hat{V} = \hat{v} - \hat{r}^* \qquad (3.10)$$

which separates the price and quantity effects. Open-market operations can be expressed as

$$-dS = dV = d\left(\frac{v}{r^*}\right) = dv \frac{1}{r^*} \qquad (3.11)$$

which indicates that the value of bonds purchased (sold) by the central bank is equal in value to the bonds sold (purchased) by the private sector. Since open-market operations cannot change the world interest rate, these transactions take place at a fixed price.

The Demand for Bonds

The total supply of bonds available to the public is held either by domestic residents or foreigners. Domestic demand for these bonds is assumed to depend on income, the interest rate, and the wealth position, while foreigners are assumed to hold any excess after domestic residents have decided on the optimal amount to hold. Thus the total demand function is

$$V = F(Y/W, r^*) W + V^* \qquad (3.12)$$

where V is now interpreted as the total public demand for bonds and V^* represents foreign holdings of domestic bonds, both in value terms.

The domestic demand function is symmetrical to the demand function for money, except that the direction of the effects of the arguments in $F(\ )$ are reversed. An increase in the ratio of income to wealth is expected to lead to a lower proportion of total wealth held in the form of bonds, while an increase in the world interest rate (equal to the domestic interest rate) is expected to have the opposite effect. Once domestic demand is determined by Y, r^*, and W, foreigners are prepared to hold any amount that is in excess supply.[g] Although it is possible that there is excess domestic demand for bonds for some values of Y, r^*, and W, it will be assumed that V^* is always positive. In any case, this is only relevant for determining the direction of foreign interest payments.

In terms of proportional changes, equation (3.12) becomes

$$\hat{V} = \lambda_{FV}[\eta_{F,\,Y/W}\hat{Y} + \eta_{F,\,r^*}\,\hat{r}^* + (1 - \eta_{F,\,Y/W})\hat{W}] + \lambda_{V^*V}\hat{V}^* \qquad (3.13)$$

where λ_{FV} and λ_{V^*V} represent the proportion of total bonds held by domestic residents and foreigners, respectively. Since $\eta_{F,\,Y/W} < 0$, an increase in wealth will unambiguously increase the demand for bonds.

Equilibrium in the Bond Market

Combining equations (3.10) and (3.13) provides us with the equilibrium condition in the bond market, namely

$$\hat{v} = \lambda_{FV}[\eta_{F,Y/W}\hat{Y} + (1 - \eta_{F,Y/W})\hat{W}]$$
$$+ (1 + \lambda_{FV}\,\eta_{F,r^*})\,\hat{r}^* + \lambda_{V^*V}\hat{V}^* \qquad (3.14)$$

The Domestic Wealth Position

In this simplified framework, domestic wealth consists of nominal money holdings and the value of domestic bonds held by domestic residents.[h] Thus

$$W = S + R + \frac{V}{r^*} - V^* \qquad (3.15a)$$

or

$$W = f(Y/W,r^*)W + F(Y/W,r^*)W \qquad (3.15b)$$

In the first part of equation (3.15a), wealth has been defined as the total supply of the two assets available to domestic residents while the second part focuses on the demand for these two assets.

From equation (3.15b), we can derive the relationship between the two demand elasticities with respect to Y/W. Dividing (3.15b) by W and differentiating yields

$$\eta_{f,\,Y/W} = -\frac{F}{f}\,\eta_{F,\,Y/W} \qquad (3.16)$$

[g]The foreign demand for domestic bonds could be written as $V^* = V^*(r - r^*)$. Perfect capital mobility implies $dV^*/d(r - r^*) \to \infty$, so that in equilibrium, $r = r^*$. But this does not determine the equilibrium value of V^*.

[h]Private residents of the SOE consider their holdings of government liabilities as "wealth" even though they have to bear the "burden" of the debt.

Similarly, the relationship between the two interest elasticities is

$$\eta_{f, r^*} = - \frac{F}{f} \, \eta_{F, r^*} \tag{3.17}$$

Focusing now on the supply side, equation (3.15a) in terms of proportional changes is

$$\hat{W} = \lambda_{SW}\hat{S} + \lambda_{RW}\hat{R} + \lambda_{VW}(\hat{v} - \hat{r}^*) - \lambda_{V^*W}\hat{V} \tag{3.18}$$

where $\lambda_{SW} = S/W$, etc. By definition, $\lambda_{SW} + \lambda_{RW} + \lambda_{VW} - \lambda_{V^*W} = 1$. Together, $\hat{S}$ and $\hat{v}$ represent open-market operations, the exogenous policy instrument available to the central bank for determining the proportion of total bonds held by itself or the public. On the other hand, $\hat{R}$ and $\hat{V}^*$ reflect the influence on domestic wealth of transactions between the small open economy and the rest of the world. There is, however, a unique relationship between these two variables. A balance-of-payments surplus involves the sum of the trade balance [B as defined by equation (2.38) in Chapter 2] and the capital account balance, the latter involving foreign purchases of domestic bonds. Thus, abstracting from interest payments to foreigners, the balance of payments per unit of time is defined as

$$R(t) - R(t - 1) = B + V^*(t) - V^*(t - 1) \tag{3.19}$$

But since we are assuming that all income is spent, $B = 0$. Thus, differentiating equation (3.19) with respect to current values only and writing the result in proportional terms, we obtain

$$\hat{R} = \frac{V^*}{R} \, \hat{V}^* \tag{3.20}$$

We now see that reserves are accumulated (decumulated) to the extent that foreigners purchase (sell) domestic bonds. Substituting (3.20) into (3.18) we obtain

$$\hat{W} = \lambda_{SW}\hat{S} + \lambda_{VW}(\hat{v} - \hat{r}^*) \tag{3.21}$$

which implies that the additions to the money supply caused by a balance-of-payments surplus merely offset the decline in the value of bonds held by domestic residents, leaving only $\hat{S}$, $\hat{v}$, and $\hat{r}^*$ to influence the level of wealth.

Equilibrium in the Asset Markets

The preceding discussion can now be summarized in the following set of equations:

$$\lambda_{SZ}\hat{S} + \lambda_{RZ}\hat{R} = \eta_{f, \, Y/W}\hat{Y} + \eta_{f, \, r^*}\hat{r}^* + (1 - \eta_{f, \, Y/W}) \, \hat{W} \tag{3.22}$$

$$\hat{v} = \lambda_{FV}[\eta_{F, \, Y/W}\hat{Y} + (1 - \eta_{F, \, Y/W})\hat{W}]$$

$$+ (1 + \lambda_{FV}\, \eta_{F,\, r^*})\hat{r}^* + (R/V)\hat{R} \qquad (3.23)$$

$$\hat{W} = \lambda_{SW}\hat{S} + \lambda_{VW}(\hat{v} - \hat{r}^*) \qquad (3.24)$$

Equations (3.22) and (3.23) specify the equilibrium conditions in the money and bond markets, respectively, while equation (3.24) stipulates the wealth constraint, all expressed in terms of proportional changes in the variables. By Walras' Law, equations (3.22) and (3.23) are not both independent. Given any exogenous shock to the system, if the equilibrium change in the money market is achieved, then equilibrium in the bond market must also be achieved. In the remainder of this section, equation (3.23) will be set aside and changes in the bond market will be determined residually.

The remaining two equations contain six variables ($\hat{S}$, $\hat{R}$, $\hat{Y}$, $\hat{r}^*$, $\hat{W}$, and $\hat{v}$). Of these, $\hat{S}$ and $\hat{v}$ together represent open-market operations; $\hat{Y}$ is exogenous to the asset markets since income is determined in the goods markets (or factor markets) and prices are assumed to be constant; while $\hat{r}^*$ is determined by changes in world bond market conditions and is therefore also exogenous to the asset markets of the SOE. Thus $\hat{R}$ and $\hat{W}$ are the endogenous variables in the system. Solving for these variables in terms of the exogenous variables, we obtain

$$\hat{W} = \lambda_{SW}\hat{S} + \lambda_{VW}(\hat{v} - \hat{r}^*) \qquad (3.24)$$

$$\hat{R} = \frac{1}{\lambda_{RZ}}\, [\eta_{f,\, Y/W}\hat{Y} + (\eta_{f,\, r^*} - (1 - \eta_{f,\, Y/W})\lambda_{VW})\hat{r}^*$$

$$+ (-\lambda_{SZ} + (1 - \eta_{f,\, Y/W})\lambda_{SW})\hat{S}$$

$$+ \lambda_{VW}(1 - \eta_{f,\, Y/W})\hat{V}] \qquad (3.25)$$

Since this is not a simultaneous system of equations, $\hat{W}$ is as indicated earlier in equation (3.24) which is merely repeated here. We can now investigate the effects on the holdings of international reserves and the domestic wealth position of three exogenous events: (1) open-market operations, (2) an increase in income, and (3) an increase in the world interest rate.

Open-Market Operations

Assume that the central bank in the SOE wishes to follow expansionary monetary policy, implying the purchase of bonds from the public. Thus $dS = -dV$ or $\hat{v} - \hat{r}^* = -(S/V)\hat{S}$. Since this policy cannot change the foreign interest rate and since income is determined in the commodity markets, $\hat{Y} = \hat{r}^* = 0$. Thus, substituting $\hat{v} = -(S/V)\hat{S}$ into equation (3.25) yields

$$\hat{R} = -(S/R)\hat{S} \qquad (3.26)$$

In terms of absolute changes in the variables, $dR/dS = -1$. There are two important interrelated implications to be derived from this result. In the first place, as originally suggested by R. A. Mundell, monetary policy in the form of open-market operations becomes inoperative when fixed exchange rates prevail in a small open economy with perfect capital mobility. An expansionary open-market operation will force the central bank into a contractionary foreign exchange transaction leaving the total monetary base unchanged. This can be seen by substituting the result of equation (3.26) into equation (3.2), from which

$$\hat{Z} = \lambda_{SZ}\hat{S} - \lambda_{RZ}(S/R)\hat{S} = 0 \qquad (3.27)$$

Secondly, sterilization operations in this environment are also impossible. An open-market operation to offset the effects of a balance-of-payments surplus or deficit will merely result in another surplus or deficit of equal size to the sterilization operation, leading to the exhaustion of one of the two assets held by the central bank. Since sterilization operations are not feasible, we can derive the significant policy conclusion that balance-of-payments disequilibrium can never be consistent with static domestic internal equilibrium since the former implies a continuing change in the supply of money, which would require constant adjustment in the demand for money. By the same token, equilibrium in the balance of payments is achieved at *any* fixed exchange rate if there is domestic equilibrium and if the world interest rate is constant. In other words, according to equation (3.25), if $\hat{Y} = \hat{r}^* = \hat{S} = \hat{v} = 0$, then $\hat{R} = 0$.

Solving now for the change in the domestic wealth position as a result of the open-market operation, we obtain

$$\hat{W} = \lambda_{SW}\hat{S} - \lambda_{VW}(S/V)\hat{S} = 0 \qquad (3.28)$$

Given the situation described above, it is not surprising to find that open-market operations do not change the level of wealth. Not even the composition of wealth has been altered. The reduction in domestic holdings of bonds caused by the open-market operation has been offset by domestic purchases of bonds from foreigners paying for them with the excess money balances provided by the central bank. In other words, in the absence of changes in either income or the world interest rate, private domestic portfolios must return to their initial positions. Only the composition of the central bank portfolio has been altered with larger amounts of bonds and fewer international reserves. In short, the open-market operation has completely bypassed the private domestic sector.

Changes in Income

We can now investigate the effects on the asset markets of an exogeneous increase in income caused by, say, increased factor supplies. As long as this increase in income is matched by an equal increase in expenditures (that is, $\hat{Y} = \hat{E}$), the trade balance will continue to be zero and the system described above will continue to hold. It may be argued that a higher level of income will lead to a higher level of *desired* wealth, implying positive savings until this goal is reached, and therefore $Y > E$. Nevertheless, we will abstract from this issue until we deal with price and exchange-rate changes where the problem becomes more clear-cut.

Solving for the changes in the two endogenous variables, the results are

$$\hat{R} = (1/\lambda_{RZ})\, \eta_{f,\, Y/W}\, \hat{Y} \tag{3.29}$$

and

$$\hat{W} = 0 \tag{3.30}$$

As a result of the higher income, domestic residents will want to hold larger money balances and fewer bonds. Since the central bank is assumed not to be prepared to provide for the increased demand for transactions balances, the economy must run a temporary balance-of-payments surplus to increase the money supply. This increase in the level of reserves is achieved when the price of domestic bonds is *temporarily* lowered as the public attempts to shift from bonds to money, the higher yield causing foreigners to buy more domestic bonds until the yield falls to the world level. In a sense, the central bank is forced to provide the extra cash balances by the requirement that it intervene in the foreign exchange market to maintain the fixed exchange rate.[16] Wealth has not changed since domestic residents have merely increased their money holdings at the expense of their bond holdings.

Changes in the World Interest Rate

An increase in the world interest rate could come about from open-market operations in the rest of the world so that foreign portfolios would then exhibit excess demand for money and excess supply of bonds. The equilibrating mechanism is an increase in the world interest rate until foreign wealth holders are satisfied with the higher supply of bonds and the lower supply of money. They cannot satisfy their demands at the existing interest rate by trading assets with the SOE because the latter is too small to meet these demands. The domestic interest rate will rise to the same extent as the world interest rate because of international arbitrage in bonds. The influence of this exogenous shock to the system can now be analyzed.

$$\hat{R} = 1/\lambda_{RZ}[\eta_{f,\, r^*} - (1 - \eta_{f,\, Y/W})\lambda_{VW}]\hat{r}^* \tag{3.31}$$

and

$$\hat{W} = -\lambda_{VW}\hat{r}^* \tag{3.32}$$

A rise in the interest rate is translated into a fall in the price of bonds, and therefore wealth declines. Also, the increased interest rate will cause domestic asset holders to shift out of money balances into bonds. In this case, they buy the bonds from foreigners, paying for them with international reserves, and thus $\hat{R} < 0$. In short, contractionary monetary policy in the rest of the world has succeeded in contracting the money supply in the small open economy as well.

The Substitutability of Assets

It has been assumed throughout that domestic and foreign bonds are perfect substitutes. However, by the nature of the system, it could be argued that domestic money and international reserves are also perfect substitutes for each other and for both types of bonds. With a constant world interest rate, bonds (both domestic and foreign) and money will always be exchanged at a fixed price between them. In addition, with a fixed exchange rate, domestic money and international money will also be exchanged at a fixed price. If all of these conditions hold true, domestic residents will have no occasion to hold money except at the exact moment that transactions take place since interest-earning bonds dominate noninterest-earning money in their portfolios. However, in the preceding analysis, a unique (nonzero) ratio of money to bonds is assumed to exist at every level of income and wealth. This is derived from the proposition that while the interest rate is exogenously determined for the SOE, investors are assumed to be faced with some uncertainty about the future level of interest rates resulting in *potential* capital gains or losses on their holdings of bonds. This condition, according to James Tobin,[17] is sufficient for optimum portfolios of risk-averters to contain both money and bonds.

Equities as a Third Asset

The introduction of a third asset, namely equities that represent the market valuation of the capital stock of the economy, has a number of potential implications for the asset market behavior discussed above. As Tobin[18] has pointed out, it is a discrepancy between the marginal efficiency of capital (MEC) and the yield on equities ("supply price of capital" in his terminology) rather than the interest rate—interpreted as the yield on bonds—that is the motivating force behind investment. As an example, if investors are prepared to hold a given number of equities at a yield below the marginal efficiency of capital, it will be profitable for firms to sell more equities, using the proceeds to buy new capital goods. In the process, the yield on equities will rise (that is, their price will fall), and the MEC will fall until they are equal, at which point further investment is not profitable. It is therefore of some interest to ask whether monetary policy in the form of open-market operations can influence the yield on equities even though it is now clear that it cannot change the yield on bonds. In order to make this question meaningful, it is necessary to assume that equities are nontradable internationally. This could be justified on some of the same grounds as those for nontradable commodities. For instance, taxes on foreign equities could be so high as to discourage investors from holding any foreign equities no matter what the relative pretax yield might be on domestic and foreign equities. If it were assumed that equities were as mobile internationally as bonds, the yield on them would be equal to the world yield on equities and the analysis would be merely repetitious.[i] The stage is now set for an analysis of domestic portfolios that contain two earning assets: one that is perfectly mobile and one that is perfectly immobile.

First, consider the supply and demand conditions in the equities market and then alter the previous analysis to reflect the existence of this new asset. Let ρ be the yield on equities. This yield is determined by

$$\rho = \frac{y_e}{V'} \tag{3.33}$$

where y_e is the stream of income derived from ownership of equities and V' represents the market value of all equities. In equilibrium, ρ must equal the marginal efficiency of capital. However, since we are only interested in determining whether monetary policy can change ρ and not what the end result is in terms of investment stimulated by the change in ρ, this constraint will not be imposed, and the number of equities, or the capital stock that the equities represent, will be held constant. Equation (3.33) can be rewritten as $V' = y_e/\rho$ which determines the *value* of the capital stock or equities for any given y_e and ρ.

The demand for equities in value terms now depends on the rate of return on equities, the yield on bonds, income, and wealth. Thus the value of existing equities is equated to the demand for them by the following equation:

$$V' = \frac{y_e}{\rho} = g(Y/W, r^*, \rho)W \tag{3.34}$$

The derivatives of the function are assumed to be $\partial g/\partial(Y/W) < 0$, $\partial g/\partial r^* < 0$ and $\partial g/\partial \rho > 0$. In other words, money, bonds, and equities are imperfect

---

[i] It would be sufficient to assume that domestic and foreign equities are imperfect substitutes, but the proposition that domestic equities are nontradable considerably simplifies the analysis.

substitutes for each other. In terms of proportional changes, equation (3.34) becomes

$$\hat{y}_e - \hat{\rho} = \eta_{g,\,Y/W}\hat{Y} + \eta_{g,\,r^*}\hat{r}^* + \eta_{g,\,\rho}\hat{\rho} + (1 - \eta_{g,\,Y/W})\,\hat{W} \qquad (3.35)$$

We must now redefine domestic wealth to include the value of equities. Thus

$$W = S + R + V - V^* + y_e/\rho \qquad (3.36)^j$$

Remembering the relationship between $\hat{R}$ and $\hat{V}^*$ through the balance of payments, proportional changes in wealth are determined by

$$\hat{W} = \lambda_{SW}\hat{S} + \lambda_{VW}\hat{V} + \lambda_{V'W}(\hat{y}_e - \hat{\rho}) \qquad (3.37)$$

Finally, the yield on equities now becomes an argument in the demand functions for money and bonds and thus equations (3.22) and (3.23) are altered to reflect this fact.

$$\lambda_{SZ}\hat{S} + \lambda_{RZ}\hat{R} = \eta_{f,\,Y/W}\hat{Y} + \eta_{f,\,r^*}\hat{r}^*$$
$$+ \eta_{f,\,\rho}\hat{\rho} + (1 - \eta_{f,\,Y/W})\hat{W} \qquad (3.38)$$

$$\hat{V} = \lambda_{FV}[\eta_{F,\,Y/W}\hat{Y} + \eta_{F,\,r^*}\,\hat{r}^* + \eta_{F,\,\rho}\hat{\rho}$$
$$+ (1 - \eta_{F,\,Y/W})\hat{W}] + (R/V)\hat{R} \qquad (3.39)$$

With three asset-equilibrium conditions, only two are now independent. Therefore, we will again drop equation (3.39). In the remaining three equations [(3.35), (3.37), and (3.38)] we have two more variables ($\hat{y}_e$ and $\hat{\rho}$) than previously. But $\hat{y}_e$ is determined in the commodities and factor markets and is therefore exogenous to the asset-market system. The three endogenous variables are now $\hat{R}$, $\hat{W}$, and $\hat{\rho}$.

We now want to determine the effect of open-market operations on the yield on equities, holding all other exogenous variables constant. Thus

$$\hat{\rho} = \frac{\lambda_{RZ}}{\Delta}\,(\lambda_{SW}\hat{S} + \lambda_{VW}\hat{V})\,(1 - \eta_{g,\,Y/W}) \qquad (3.40)$$

where $\Delta = \lambda_{RZ}[1 + \eta_{g,\,\rho} - \lambda_{V'W}(1 - \eta_{g,\,Y/W})] > 0$. Open-market operations are once more depicted as $\hat{V} = -(S/V)\hat{S}$. Therefore $\hat{\rho} = 0$.

This result proves that even if nontraded equities are included in domestic portfolios, monetary policy is again helpless in influencing the variable that, at least conceptually, is crucial in determining aggregate demand. After the open-market operation, domestic residents have replenished their bond holdings by buying them from foreigners, paying for them with the excess money balances. Since portfolios have returned to their original

---

[j]In this section, V defines the *value* of bonds issued by the government. Since r^* will be held constant, it is not necessary to divide V into its quantity and price components.

levels and neither rate of return (that is, r^* and ρ) has changed, wealth also remains unaltered.[19]

Since open-market operations in a model with nontradable equities are unable to change the money supply, we can conclude once more that monetary policy in a small open economy with fixed exchange rates is ineffective as a stabilization policy instrument. In view of this conclusion, I will revert to a model that includes only money and bonds as assets.

Flexible Exchange Rates and the Asset Markets

Once the possibility of changes in the exchange rate are introduced into the analysis of the asset markets, four important implications arise. These are: (1) the impact of changes in the exchange rate on the price level, (2) the exogeneity of the money supply, (3) the potential effects on the perfect substitutability of domestic and foreign bonds and (4) changes in the price level that cause a discrepancy between actual and desired wealth. Consider each of these points in turn.

In the first place, if foreign prices of tradables are constant, a change in the exchange rate is the *only* means by which the domestic price level is altered. This proposition can be derived from the analysis in Chapter 2. Substituting equations (2.20), (2.21) and (2.51) into equation (2.37) we obtain

$$\hat{p} = \theta_x \hat{\pi} + \theta_m \hat{\pi} + \theta_n \hat{\pi} = \hat{\pi} \qquad (3.41)$$

since $\theta_x + \theta_m + \theta_n = 1$. In this case, it is necessary to consider the effects of price changes on the various asset demands.

Secondly, if a truly flexible exchange rate regime is allowed to exist, domestic intervention in the foreign exchange market is precluded by the "rules of the game" and therefore the money supply becomes an exogenous variable in the system. In other words, $\hat{R} = 0$ by definition and open-market operations do not have offsetting effects on the money supply through changes in the level of international reserves. By the same token, a temporary nonzero trade balance must now exist whenever capital flows are created by any tendency for the domestic interest rate to deviate from the world interest rate. Thus, equilibrium in the foreign exchange market is established when a trade surplus (deficit) exactly offsets a capital-account deficit (surplus). This relationship can be written as

$$B + \dot{V}^* = 0 \qquad (3.42)$$

where $B = Y - E$ is the trade balance as represented by the difference between income and expenditures and $\dot{V}^*$ represents foreign purchases of domestic bonds, per unit of time (that is, $V^* = dV^*/dt$). But, asset-market equilibrium requires that $\dot{V}^* = 0$, so that in equation (3.42), $B = 0$.[k]

Thirdly, flexible exchange rates will render the perfect substitutability of domestic and foreign bonds in doubt. In particular, a depreciation of the domestic currency results in a capital loss to foreigners holding domestic bonds. (If domestic residents held foreign bonds in their portfolios, they would experience a capital gain.) Thus, if the depreciation is anticipated, foreigners will attempt to rid themselves of domestic bonds in order to prevent such a capital loss. This means that speculative capital flows, which so far have been absent from the analysis, would have to be taken into account. Therefore, in order to maintain the assumption of perfect substitutability of domestic and foreign bonds, it is asserted that changes in the exchange rate are not anticipated and therefore capital gains and losses are accepted passively by foreign holders of domestic bonds. This may not be too unrealistic since foreign holdings of domestic bonds represent a miniscule proportion of total foreign wealth. However, in the next section, covered interest arbitrage, which is a hedge against changes in the exchange rate, will be considered to be a more appropriate alternative.

Finally, a change in the exchange rate will affect the real value of wealth (through the resulting change in the price level as noted above) and to the extent that wealth holders desire this value to remain constant (or more generally in some proportion to real income), desired nominal wealth will rise (fall) after a depreciation (appreciation) of the exchange rate. For W/p to remain constant, it is necessary that nominal wealth change according to

$$\hat{W} = \hat{p} = \hat{\pi} \tag{3.43}$$

This equation stipulates the change in *desired* wealth. The source of *actual* changes in wealth is determined by

$$\hat{W} = \lambda_{SW}\hat{S} + \lambda_{VW}\hat{V} - \lambda_{V^*W}\hat{V}^* \tag{3.44}$$

which differs from equation (3.21) where changes in R and V^* offset each other.[1]

The demand function for money now becomes

$$Z/p = f\left(\frac{Y/p}{W/p}, r^*\right) W/p \tag{3.45}$$

As can be seen from this equation, the introduction of variable prices does

---

[k]This does not deny the possibility of a one-time change in V^* in conjunction with a temporary nonzero trade balance.

[1]If desired wealth increased because of increases in world prices of tradables, rather than because of a change in the exchange rate, the money supply again becomes endogenous and equation (3.21) is the appropriate constraint.

not affect the demand for money. Multiplying through by p results in the duplication of equation (3.4). It should be noted that the *nominal* world interest rate remains the appropriate argument in the demand function since rising prices affect the future purchasing power of money and bonds equally, leaving unaffected the relative rate of return of the two assets. In terms of proportional changes, the equilibrium condition in the money market becomes

$$\hat{S} = \eta_{f,\,Y/W}\hat{Y} + \eta_{f,\,r^*}\hat{r}^* + (1 - \eta_{f,\,Y/W})\hat{W} \qquad (3.46)$$

In this equation, only changes in central bank holdings of government bonds affect the money supply since international reserves are assumed not to exist.[m]

The change in nominal income can be decomposed into quantity and price changes, so that $\hat{Y} = \hat{y} + \hat{p}$, where y is real income. This component is still determined in the commodity or factor markets and thus is exogenous to the asset markets. It has been assumed earlier that, in equilibrium, income and expenditures are equal. However, after an exogenous shock to the system, there is an intervening disequilibrium period when this condition does not hold true. This disequilibrium arises because domestic residents want to accumulate wealth after a depreciation of the currency caused by the initial shock to the system. In order to do this, they must retrieve some of the bonds held by foreigners which gives rise to a deficit in the capital account. Because of the flexible exchange rate regime, they must therefore achieve a surplus in the trade account, or income must exceed expenditures. After they have reached the new desired level of wealth, saving ceases, or income is once again equal to expenditures. Therefore, the following results must be viewed as final effects on the system after a once-and-for-all open-market operation.

Combining equations (3.43) and (3.44) together with equation (3.46) allows us to solve for the two endogenous variables in the system (that is, $\hat{\pi}$ and $\hat{V}^*$).[n] Holding the foreign interest rate constant, we obtain the following solutions:

$$\hat{\pi} = \hat{S} \qquad (3.47)$$

$$\hat{V}^* = 1/\lambda_{V^*W}[(\lambda_{SW} - 1)\hat{S} + \lambda_{VW}\hat{V}] \qquad (3.48)$$

Since open-market operations imply $\hat{V} = -(S/V)\hat{S}$, equation (3.48) reduces to $\hat{V}^* = -[1/(\lambda_{V^*W})]\hat{S}$. Thus if expansionary monetary policy is pursued, $\hat{\pi} > 0$, indicating a depreciation of the domestic currency or a higher price for the foreign currency, and there will be a deficit in the capital account. These results can be explained in terms of the following sequence of events.

---

[m]If the central bank holds international reserves even if flexible exchange rates prevail, the change in the money supply is equal to $\lambda_{sz}\hat{S}$.

[n]Since $\hat{\pi} = \hat{p}$, we are also implicitly solving for the change in the price level.

Immediately after the open-market operation, domestic residents will want to convert the excess money balances into bonds in order to return to the initial equilibrium. They purchase these bonds from foreigners and the resulting incipient deficit in the capital account causes a depreciation of the domestic currency and a higher price level. Because of the lower real value of wealth, the economy will reduce its expenditures below its income so as to recoup its wealth position. As wealth is being accumulated, it must be held in money and bonds and more of both assets will be demanded. Ultimately, the proportional increase in wealth is equal to the percentage change in the exchange rate as stipulated by equation (3.43). The increase in the demand for money is satisfied by the original change in the money supply as indicated by equation (3.46), while the increased demand for bonds is satisfied by the temporary surplus in the trade balance. In the new equilibrium, after the capital flows have disappeared and the trade balance is once more zero, the exchange rate will be stabilized at a higher level since no further pressure is exerted in either direction.

In this world of full employment and flexible prices, it is not surprising to find that expansionary monetary policy has really affected only the price level.[o] In the next chapter, where unemployed resources can exist in equilibrium, monetary policy will be found to influence both income and prices as long as flexible exchange rates prevail, making it into an effective stabilization-policy instrument.

The Forward Market and Flexible Exchange Rates

When a flexible exchange rate system is allowed to operate, it may be unrealistic to assume that investors are so myopic that changes in the exchange rate will generate no anticipations about future changes in that rate. Yet Mundell works within this framework. He states that "existing exchange rates are expected to persist indefinitely (even when the exchange rate is not pegged) and . . . spot and forward exchange rates are identical. All the complications associated with speculation, the forward market, and exchange-rate margins are thereby assumed not to exist."[20] In fact, investors are much more likely to take the view that exchange rate risks do exist and therefore hedge their foreign investments in the forward market in order to make these investments riskless. In these circumstances, perfect capital mobility no longer dictates that domestic and world interest rates be equal, but instead that the *covered* domestic interest rate

---

[o]Contractionary monetary policy would lead to an appreciation of the exchange rate, a lower price level, a temporary excess of expenditures over income, a trade deficit and a capital-account surplus.

be equal to the world interest rate. That is, the domestic interest rate can be higher (lower) than the world interest rate as long as the premium (discount) on forward contracts offsets this interest differential. When this condition is fulfilled, foreign investors will be satisfied with their holdings of domestic bonds since the net yields on domestic and world bonds have been equalized.

Victor Argy and M. G. Porter[21] have investigated a model of a small open economy incorporating such hedged investments and have found that exogenous shocks to the system produce results that are at some variance with those derived by Mundell. In view of the fact that the previous section was based on the same assumption as Mundell's, it is now appropriate to consider the same model of the asset markets with the added characteristic that foreign investments are hedged in the forward market.

In this case, the amount of domestic bonds held by foreigners is determined by

$$V^* = V^*\left(r - r^* - \frac{\pi_f - \pi}{\pi} \right) \qquad (3.49)$$

where r is the domestic interest rate and π_f is the price of foreign exchange in the forward market. The entire expression in the brackets is equal to the covered interest differential. Perfect capital mobility now implies that

$$dV^*/d\left(r - r^* - \frac{\pi_f - \pi}{\pi} \right) \to \infty \qquad (3.50)$$

In other words, V^* takes on an equilibrium value when

$$r - r^* - \frac{\pi_f - \pi}{\pi} = 0 \qquad (3.51)$$

Argy and Porter assume that speculators dominate arbitrageurs in the forward market so that the forward rate is equal to the expected future spot rate.[22] This assertion is based on the presumption that there are no constraints on the amount of forward commitments by speculators and that there exist uniformly held expectations about the future spot rate. They then argue that the future spot rate is determined by

$$\pi_e = \pi(t) + \alpha[\pi(t) - \pi(t - 1)] \qquad (3.52)$$

The parameter α is the coefficient of expectations, indicating that speculators extrapolate the past trend in exchange rates in determining the future spot rate. If $\alpha > 0$, expectations are elastic, while if $\alpha < 0$, then expectations are inelastic. The case where $\alpha = 0$ is consistent with Mundell's assumption. Since $\pi_e = \pi_f$ by assumption, equation (3.52) can be substituted into (3.51) so that

$$r - r^* - \alpha\left[\frac{\pi(t) - \pi(t - 1)}{\pi(t)} \right] = 0 \qquad (3.53)$$

From this equation, it can be seen that there will be a divergence between the domestic and world interest rates as long as the exchange rate is moving over time. Thus, starting from a position of $r = r^*$, implying that $\pi(t) = \pi(t - 1)$, assume an exogenous event that increases the exchange rate. In the next period, $\pi(t + 1) > \pi(t)$, and therefore $r > r^*$, if $\alpha < 0$. But, if the exchange rate now remains at the new higher level, the premium on forward contracts will disappear, leading again to the equality of the domestic and world interest rates. It can therefore be concluded that, even if foreign investments are hedged in the forward market, the domestic interest rate can diverge from the world interest rate only in the short run. In the long run, the domestic interest rate is constrained to be equal to the world interest rate, as in the case of fixed exchange rates.[p]

Nevertheless, it is worth exploring the *temporary* equilibrium in the asset markets generated by some exogenous change in the system such as an open-market operation. Differentiating (3.53) totally, we obtain

$$dr - dr^* - \alpha \left[\frac{\pi(t - 1)d\pi(t) - \pi(t)d\pi(t - 1)}{\pi(t)^2} \right] = 0 \qquad (3.54)$$

Assuming that initially $r = r^*$ and therefore $\pi(t) - \pi(t - 1) = 0$, equation (3.54) can be rewritten as

$$r(\hat{r} - \hat{r}^*) - \alpha[\hat{\pi}(t) - \hat{\pi}(t - 1)] = 0 \qquad (3.55)$$

Because investments in domestic bonds are a small proportion of the total world supply of bonds, r^* is exogenous and it is assumed that $\hat{r}^* = 0$.

Equation (3.46) which describes the equilibrium condition in the money market must be altered to reflect the fact that the domestic interest rate is now the appropriate variable in the demand function. Thus

$$\hat{S} = \eta_{f,Y/W}(\hat{y} + \hat{p}) + \eta_{f,r}\hat{r} + (1 - \eta_{f,Y/W})\hat{W} \qquad (3.56)$$

I again assume that real income is constant (that is, $\hat{y} = 0$), and that $\hat{W} = \hat{\pi} = \hat{p}$ to reflect the change in desired wealth caused by a change in the exchange rate. Thus equation (3.56) becomes

$$\hat{S} = \eta_{f,r}\hat{r} + \hat{\pi}(t) \qquad (3.57)$$

Equations (3.55) and (3.57) contain two endogenous variables, $\hat{r}$ and $\hat{\pi}(t)$, and two exogenous variables, $\hat{S}$ and $\hat{\pi}(t - 1)$. Solving for these variables we obtain

$$\hat{r} = \frac{\alpha\hat{S} + \alpha\hat{\pi}(t - 1)}{\alpha\eta_{f,r} + r} \qquad (3.58)$$

---

[p]This is only true for the case where the exchange rate is constant in equilibrium. It is possible, however, for the exchange rate to undergo continuous change, in which case the domestic interest rate would diverge from the world interest rate even in the long run.

and

$$\hat{\pi}(t) = \frac{r\hat{S} - \alpha\eta_{f,r}\hat{\pi}(t-1)}{\alpha\eta_{f,r} + r} \tag{3.59}$$

We now want to investigate the effects of expansionary monetary policy ($\hat{S} > 0$) on the system.[q] Therefore, assuming $\alpha \neq 0$, while $\hat{\pi}(t-1) = 0$ and dividing (3.58) and (3.59) by α yields

$$\hat{r} = \frac{\hat{S}}{\eta_{f,r} + r/\alpha} \tag{3.60}$$

and

$$\hat{\pi}(t) = \frac{\hat{S}}{\eta_{f,r}\alpha/r + 1} \tag{3.61}$$

As can be seen from these expressions, the value of the parameter α is crucial in determining the direction of change of $\hat{r}$ and $\hat{\pi}(t)$. If expectations are inelastic (that is, $\alpha < 0$), then $\hat{r} < 0$ while $\hat{\pi}(t) > 0$. That is, expansionary open-market operations will lead to a decrease in the domestic interest rate, a result which is consistent with the traditional analysis. Foreigners will sell domestic bonds and since this is a capital outflow, the domestic currency will depreciate. At the same time, foreigners are buying the domestic currency in the forward market, appreciating its value in that market. Temporary equilibrium will be reestablished when the premium on forward contracts (dictated essentially by the expectations of speculators) equals the interest differential. In other words, the domestic interest rate must fall far enough so that the hedged yield on domestic bonds equals the world interest rate. These results will still hold true if expectations are elastic (that is, $\alpha > 0$), the necessary and sufficient condition being that $\eta_{f,r} + r/\alpha < 0$.

The important point to note is that now the domestic monetary authorities have some short-run control over the domestic interest rate, making monetary policy a potentially effective stabilization instrument.[r] This conclusion is not at odds with that of Mundell; however his argument did not require a change in the domestic interest rate, the change in income being dictated only by the change in the exchange rate. While fiscal policy

---

[q]The offsetting decline in V is not shown, but this involves $\hat{V} = -(S/V)\hat{S}$ which, when substituted into equation (3.44) dictates that the actual change in wealth is determined by $\hat{W} = -\lambda_{V^*W}\hat{V}^*$. But we know that the actual change will equal the desired change, $\hat{W} = \hat{\pi}$.

[r]Temporary changes in the supply price of capital are now possible. Therefore, the conclusions in the section, "Equities as a Third Asset," hold only in the case of fixed exchange rates or for flexible exchange rates in the long run. However, the equities market will not be reintroduced at this stage or in later chapters because the investment goods market is not a necessary component of a stabilization-policy model. But, see J. P. Harkness[23] for this type of model.

has not been analyzed in this chapter, it is nevertheless worth mentioning that Argy and Porter have found that, under flexible exchange rates, a change in government expenditures does have effects on income, whereas Mundell came to the opposite conclusion. This dispute arises because of the conflicting views about the role of the forward market in their respective models. While this dispute can only be resolved with an appeal to empirical evidence, the assumption made by Argy and Porter has greater generality and will therefore be incorporated in the policy model of the next chapter.

Interest Payments on the Government Debt

Even though the government is assumed to be in a constant debt position, it has a role to play in the economy since it must pay interest on this debt to the holders of its obligations. These payments will alter a number of equations both in the commodity and factor markets in Chapter 2 and the asset markets in this chapter. Although it is not intended to rework the entire preceding analysis with this added variable. it is necessary to mention at least those areas that are affected by its introduction. First we must specify the payments received by each sector.[s] (See Table 3-7.) In calculating the interest payments, it is assumed again that domestic and world interest rates coincide. Of the total, the central bank is presumed to repay to the government its interest earnings equal to r^*S.[t] For the rest, the government must impose taxes so as to retain a balanced budget. For our purposes, it is assumed that these are lump-sum taxes which are equal to $\Gamma = r^*V$. These taxes are imposed only on domestic residents, otherwise foreigners would be discouraged from holding domestic bonds.

These interest payments and the taxes collected by the government change the income and expenditure equations derived in Chapter 2. For expositional simplicity, it is assumed that domestic residents receive the entire amount of interest payments due to the public (r^*V) and that they in turn expend some of their income to pay foreigners their share of the interest (r^*V^*). In addition, the lump-sum taxes are subtracted from income. The revised equations are now

$$Y = p_xQ_x + p_mQ_m + p_nQ_n + r^*V - \Gamma \qquad (3.62)^u$$

---

[s]Since bonds are consols, the holder of one bond receives one unit of the domestic currency as an interest payment Private individuals, for instance, will therefore receive total interest payments equal to v, the number of bonds they hold. But since $v(1/r^*) = V$ according to equation (3.10), this amount is equal to r^*V.

[t]It appears to be generally true that central banks return any net profits on their operations to their Treasuries.

[u]Since $r^*V - \Gamma = 0$, equation (3.62) is really the same as (2.32).

Table 3-7
Interest Payments on the Government Debt

Institution	Interest Payment Received
Central Bank	r^*S
Public	r^*V
domestic residents	$r^*(V - V^*)$
foreigners	r^*V^*
Total	$r^*(S + V)$

and

$$E = p_x A_x + p_m A_m + p_n A_n + r^* V^* \qquad (3.63)$$

In terms of proportional changes, $\hat{Y}$ and $\hat{E}$ remain as specified by equations (2.33) and (2.35), respectively, since the amounts added through interest payments and taxes remain constant, but the shares, as expressed by the θ's, no longer add to unity.

Now defining the balance on current account as the trade balance plus net interest payments to foreigners, we obtain

$$B' = Y - E = p_x(Q_x - A_x) + p_m(Q_m - A_m) - r^* V^* \qquad (3.64)$$

For $B' = 0$, it is necessary that net trade in goods be positive to offset the interest payments to foreigners. As long as domestic residents are satisfied with their present wealth position, they will spend their entire income (including interest receipts). If, in addition, foreigners do not use their interest receipts to accumulate additional domestic bonds, there will be no effect on asset markets.

If, however, the government decides to finance the interest payments with new issues of securities (that is, a government deficit) asset markets will be affected. The issue of securities necessary to finance the interest payments is determined by $\hat{V} = r^*$. This puts upward pressure on the interest rate, resulting in foreign purchases of domestic bonds. These capital inflows reduce domestic wealth but the bonds issued by the government restore the wealth position to the old level. Nevertheless, the analysis is somewhat more complicated than depicted here since income will rise as interest payments increase, leading to larger desired wealth holdings and increased transactions balances at the expense of bond holdings. These issues will be dealt with more directly in the next chapter where deficit financing of government expenditures plays a crucial role. It is sufficient for our purposes here to determine that interest payments financed by taxes tend to have their impact on the commodity markets, while deficit financing tends to require readjustment in both commodity and asset markets.

Notes

1. R. A. Mundell, "Capital Mobility and Stabilization Policy Under Fixed and Flexible Exchange Rates," *Canadian Journal of Economics and Political Science* 29 (1963): 475-85; ———, "A Reply: Capital Mobility and Size," *Canadian Journal of Economics and Political Science* 30 (1964): 421-31.

2. Victor Argy and M. G. Porter, "The Forward Exchange Market and the Effects of Domestic and External Disturbances Under Alternative Exchange Rate Systems," *International Monetary Fund Staff Papers* 19 (1972): 503-32.

3. T. F. Dernburg, "Exchange Rates and Co-ordinated Stabilization Policy," *Canadian Journal of Economics* 3 (1970): 1-13.

4. M. F. J. Prachowny, "The Effectiveness of Stabilization Policy in a Small Open Economy," *Weltwirtschaftliches Archiv* 109 (1973): 214-31.

5. Akira Takayama, "The Effects of Fiscal and Monetary Policies Under Flexible and Fixed Exchange Rates," *Canadian Journal of Economics* 2 (1969): 190-209.

6. James Tobin, "A General Equilibrium Approach to Monetary Theory," *Journal of Money, Credit and Banking* 1 (1969):15-29.

7. H. M. Markowitz, *Portfolio Selection: Efficient Diversification of Investments*, New York, John Wiley and Sons, 1959.

8. James Tobin, "Liquidity Preference as Behaviour Towards Risk," *Review of Economic Studies* 25 (1958): 65-86.

9. For a recent survey of the current state of portfolio theory, see W. J. Baumol, *Portfolio Theory: The Selection of Asset Combinations*, New York, McCaleb-Seiler Publishing Company, 1970.

10. Tobin, "A General Equilibrium Approach to Monetary Theory," p. 16.

11. Mundell, "Capital Mobility and Stabilization Policy Under Fixed and Flexible Exchange Rates," p. 475.

12. Ibid.

13. R. E. Caves and G. L. Reuber, *Capital Transfers and Economic Policy: Canada, 1951-1962*, Cambridge, Mass., Harvard University Press, 1971, p. 2.

14. See Tobin, "A General Equilibrium Approach to Monetary Theory," p. 20, for further discussion of this formulation of the transactions demand for money.

15. See R. W. Jones, "The Structure of Simple General Equilibrium Models," *Journal of Political Economy* 73 (1965): 565-66, for a discussion of this problem.

16. This result is in conformity with that derived by R. A. Mundell. See his *International Economics*, New York, The Macmillan Company, 1968, Ch. 9. He argues that, contrary to Keynesian conclusions, economic growth leads to a balance-of-payments surplus.

17. Tobin, "Liquidity Preference as Behaviour Towards Risk."

18. James Tobin, "An Essay on Principles of Debt Management," in Commission on Money and Credit, *Fiscal and Debt Management Policies*, Englewood Cliffs, N.J., Prentice-Hall, 1963, pp. 143-218.

19. Tobin, on the other hand, found that in a closed economy where the stocks of money and bonds are exogenous and where the interest rate is allowed to adjust, open-market operations do in fact influence the supply price of capital. See "A General Equilibrium Approach to Monetary Theory."

20. Mundell, "Capital Mobility and Stabilization Policy Under Fixed and Flexible Exchange Rates," p. 475-76.

21. Argy and Porter, "The Forward Exchange Market."

22. Ibid., p. 508.

23. J. P. Harkness, *Monetary and Fiscal Policy in Closed and Open Economies–The Portfolio Approach*, unpublished Ph.D. dissertation, Queen's University, Kingston, Canada, 1969.

4

The Effectiveness of Monetary and Fiscal Policies as Stabilization Instruments

Introduction

The previous two chapters dealt with the special characteristics of the commodity, factor, and asset markets of a small, open economy. Taken together, they represent the complete structure of the relevant markets of such an economy. It is important to note at this point that the preceding analysis was predicated on the assumption that all these markets adjusted smoothly and completely to exogenous shocks. In such an environment, active macroeconomic policy is both unnecessary and undesirable. But aberrations from equilibrium may not be temporary or self-correcting, even for an SOE. In particular, an SOE may find itself in a situation where, for one reason or another, unemployment is consistent with equilibrium (except in the labor market). Since this unemployment cannot be eliminated without aggregate demand policy on the part of the authorities of the SOE, it is useful to focus on the role played by the traditional instruments of stabilization policy: open-market operations, representing the single most important tool of monetary policy, and deficit spending on the part of the government, representing fiscal policy.

A small open economy is forced to operate, as we have learned from R. A. Mundell,[1] in a constrained policy environment. He found that monetary policy is ineffective as a stabilization instrument under a regime of fixed exchange rates while fiscal policy is ineffective if exchange rates are flexible. While small open economies share with their larger counterparts some of the same ills, such as unemployment and/or inflation, requiring the judicious application of stabilization policies, the effectiveness of these stabilization instruments differs markedly for SOEs. Because of this generic difference, it is to economies such as these, and not to larger or closed economies, that the analysis of this chapter is devoted. The extremity of the assumptions, discussed in the previous two chapters, is such as to make the analysis totally inapplicable to countries such as the United States. The analysis is also irrelevant for small underdeveloped countries where the tools of monetary and fiscal policies are not as sophisticated as required by the assumptions of the model (e.g., perfect capital mobility). The purpose of this chapter then is to investigate the effectiveness of stabilization policies in the constrained environment faced by SOEs. In particular, it is proposed to reexamine Mundell's conclusions about the effectiveness of monetary and fiscal policies under fixed and flexible exchange rates and to show that under flexible exchange rates an optimum policy combination exists that eliminates the trade-off between price increases and unemployment—an occurrence not possible, even theoretically, for closed economies.

As is common in these stabilization-policy models, continuous growth in factor supplies and therefore output is assumed not to exist.[2] Consequently, the model will be presented in terms of comparative statics. While the passage of time is usually irrelevant in this type of analysis, to the extent that there are lags in the adjustment from one equilibrium to another after an initial shock to the system, the effects on the endogenous variables depend on how much time has elapsed. Therefore, it is possible to generate both "impact" and "full-equilibrium" solutions. The impact effects of monetary or fiscal policy are those which occur after an initial period of arbitrary length, while the full-equilibrium effects are those obtained after sufficient time has passed for the economic system to settle down to a new, final equilibrium. Although these two solutions would generate two points on the time path from one equilibrium to the next, the analysis is not strictly dynamic in nature, unless that time path happens to be linear. In any case, only the impact effects of stabilization policy will be considered in this chapter, since, as will be argued below, the full-equilibrium effects are irrelevant unless the disequilibrium in the labor market can be assumed to be permanent.

Before proceeding with the construction of the model and testing for policy effectiveness, we must set the stage by investigating the conditions under which an underemployment equilibrium is possible and by outlining the operational characteristics of monetary and fiscal policies.

The Supply of Tradables and Nontradables in an Underemployment Equilibrium

In an economy, where all prices (including the rental rates of factors of production) are flexible, equilibrium will result in the full utilization of all resources. Even if the prices of the two tradable commodities, exportables and importables, are fixed in world markets and the exchange rate is held constant, full employment is still realized if the price of nontradables and rental rates are allowed to adjust. Under these circumstances, there is no requirement for stabilization policy as is evident from the analysis in Chapter 2. Thus, in order to make stabilization policy purposeful, it is necessary to conceive of a model that allows for equilibrium to be established inside the economy's transformation curve.

To facilitate the analysis of this phenomenon, it is convenient first of all to aggregate exportables and importables into one category called tradables. This is a legitimate procedure as long as the world prices of exportables and importables move together. Although the factor intensities of the two remaining goods (that is, tradables and nontradables) are now in doubt, this loss of information is not crucial as long as factor supplies, taxes, and tariffs are held constant. The production side of the model (still assuming full-employment equilibrium) becomes

$$a_{Lt}Q_t + a_{Ln}Q_n = L \tag{4.1}$$

$$a_{Tt}Q_t + a_{Tn}Q_n = T \tag{4.2}$$

$$a_{Lt}w + a_{Tt}r = p_t = \pi p_t^* \tag{4.3}$$

$$a_{Ln}w + a_{Tn}r = p_n \tag{4.4}$$

where Q_t and Q_n represent the output of tradables and nontradables, respectively; L and T are the two factors of production, labor and land; p_t and p_n, are the domestic prices of the two goods; w and r represent the rental rates of labor and land; π is the exchange rate; p_t^* is the world price of tradables in a numeraire currency and the a_{ij}'s represent the input requirements for a unit of output. These a_{ij}'s can be related to those in the three-good model of Chapter 2 in the following way:

$$a_{Lt} = a_{Lx} \frac{Q_x}{Q_x + Q_m} + a_{Lm} \frac{Q_m}{Q_x + Q_m} \tag{4.5}$$

$$a_{Tt} = a_{Tx} \frac{Q_x}{Q_x + Q_m} + a_{Tm} \frac{Q_m}{Q_x + Q_m} \tag{4.6}$$

where Q_x and Q_m represent the output of exportables and importables, respectively. The two input coefficients in the tradable sector are weighted averages of the input coefficients of exportables and importables. The resulting equations of change are

$$\lambda_{Lt}\hat{Q}_t + \lambda_{Ln}\hat{Q}_n = \hat{L} + \delta_L(\hat{w} - \hat{r}) \tag{4.7}$$

$$\lambda_{Tt}\hat{Q}_t + \lambda_{Tn}\hat{Q}_n = \hat{T} - \delta_T(\hat{w} - \hat{r}) \tag{4.8}$$

$$\theta_{Lt}\hat{w} + \theta_{Tt}\hat{r} = \hat{p}_t^* + \hat{\pi} \tag{4.9}$$

$$\theta_{Ln}\hat{w} + \theta_{TN}\hat{r} = \hat{p}_n \tag{4.10}$$

where the λ's and θ's are similar transforms of the a_{ij}'s as in Chapter 2, while δ_L and δ_T are also defined on p. 17 in Chapter 2. In the three-commodity model of that chapter, the world prices of exportables and importables together with the exchange rate were sufficient to determine the rates of return to the two factors (w and r), which in turn determined the price of nontradables. However, the equilibrium outputs of the three commodities required a further condition to close the system, namely the demand for the nontradable. In the present two-commodity model, I choose to make the prices of tradables and nontradables exogenous to the production sector. Any changes in these prices determine $\hat{w}$ and $\hat{r}$ (with $\hat{\pi} = 0$) and if $\hat{L} = \hat{T} = 0$, then $\hat{Q}_t$ and $\hat{Q}_n$ are determined. With this in mind, it is possible to truncate the model by specifying the supplies of the two goods in terms of their relative prices only. Hence

$$Q_t = Q_t(p_t/p_n) \tag{4.11}$$

$$Q_n = Q_n(p_t/p_n) \tag{4.12}$$

These equations imply that the economy is moving along a transformation curve, its position fixed by the availability of factor supplies, while the movement along it depends only on changes in relative prices. Given the slope of the budget line, equilibrium is established where $dQ_n/dQ_t = -p_t/p_n$. Full employment is achieved as long as *relative* prices are allowed to adjust. Even if p_t is held constant, because world prices of tradables and the exchange rate are fixed, a point on the transformation curve can always be reached as long as p_n can rise or fall sufficiently.

Stabilization policy has no role to play in this type of framework. The application of fiscal policy, for instance, through government expenditures on nontradables would merely result in higher prices and expanded output of nontradables, but at the expense of tradables. Stabilization policy only makes sense in an environment where, in its absence, aggregate demand falls short of the output available from the full utilization of all resources. It is therefore crucial to design the model to allow for unemployed factors to exist in an equilibrium that contains no governmental action. This is acheived by respecifying the supply equations of the two goods so that

$$Q_t = Q_t (p_t/p_n^\sigma) \tag{4.13}$$

$$Q_n = Q_n(p_n/p_t^\sigma) \tag{4.14}$$

where $\sigma < 1$. If the economy has sufficient unemployed resources, the output of tradables could expand without sacrificing any output of nontradables, and vice versa when aggregate demand is increased by government policy. In this case $\sigma = 0$ and

$$Q_t = Q_t(p_t) \tag{4.15}$$

$$Q_n = Q_n(p_n) \tag{4.16}$$

These then are partial equilibrium supply functions where it is assumed that $dQ_t/dp_t > 0$ and $dQ_n/dp_n > 0$. There are intermediate cases as well, where $0 < \sigma < 1$, involving increased output of one commodity accommodated by a reduction in the output of the other commodity and increased use of idle resources.[a]

What is the source of this underemployment equilibrium? In the Keynesian tradition, it is postulated that wages are "sticky", if not completely rigid, a situation which will lead to some unemployment if the wage is not at the equilibrium level and if the other factor of production (that is, land), although always fully employed, is unable to move from one industry to the other.[b] It could be argued that this unemployment is voluntary in some sense, but debating this issue is not very fruitful if policy-makers are convinced that any unemployment (whatever its cause) beyond some irreducible minimum requires active intervention in the economy. Also, we need not deal with the specific cause of the wage rigidity, which may be the result of union bargaining power, imperfect information, or lack of mobility, as long as policy-makers are either unable or unwilling to eliminate the rigidity.

Both the wage rigidity and the immobility of cooperating factors involve a time dimension. While policy-makers may be convinced that active intervention in the economy is necessary, whether wages are only temporarily sticky or permanently rigid or whether factor immobility is temporary or permanent, the degree of intervention and its length depend very much on how quickly or slowly self-correcting adjustments take place. If the rigidities in the economy are likely to last into the foreseeable future, then presumably policy-makers will want to know what the full-equilibrium effects are of any changes in monetary or fiscal policies (that is, the changes in the endogenous variables in the system after all adjustments, except the wage rate, have ceased). If, on the other hand, the rigidities are expected to be eliminated before all the other adjustments are complete, policy-makers will likely provide a stimulus to aggregate demand only temporarily since full employment will be achieved after the rigidities are removed without any further intervention on the part of the authorities. In this case, they are interested only in determining the initial or impact effects of policy changes.

In the "real" world, permanent rigidities in the economy are not a sustainable assumption. Instead, it will be assumed that wages are sticky

---

[a]In addition, it is possible to specify that the parameter σ differs between the two sectors.

[b]The assumption of a "sticky" rental rate of land could be substituted for the assumption about its immobility. In that case, land would also be underutilized. However, treating labor as the variable factor and land as the fixed factor in short-run production decisions is most relevant in this context, as will be seen shortly. To show that immobility of land is a necessary (but not sufficient) condition for this type of model, we can solve equations (4.9) and (4.10), treating the right-hand sides as exogenous. In addition to $\hat{w} = 0$, it is assumed that $\hat{p}_t^* = \hat{\pi} = 0$. Thus, $\theta_{Tt}\hat{r} = 0$ and $\theta_{Tn}\hat{r} = \hat{p}_n$. These solutions are inconsistent with each other unless it is stipulated that there are separate rates of return to land in the two industries, a situation which will arise if land is immobile.

just long enough for policy-makers to be convinced that the costs of lags in the adjustment to an equilibrium wage are too burdensome on the economy (particularly on those who are unemployed in the interim) and also long enough for the initial effects of policy changes to be consistent with the assumption of wage rigidity. In this context, only the impact effects of stabilization policy are relevant.[3]

It may be suggested that a small, open economy need never suffer from unemployment for lack of sufficient aggregate demand since it is able to sell as much as it wants of its tradable commodity in world markets. But with rigid wages and declining marginal productivity of labor, profit-maximizing producers of tradables will not expand production and thus increase the use of factors unless the price of the product rises. But as price-takers they cannot hope for such a result and make their production decision on the basis of the externally determined price. This points to the crux of the problem: only stabilization policy can increase the domestic price of tradables and nontradables which in turn encourages larger output of both commodities and therfore generates a reduction in idle resources.

The Instruments of Stabilization Policy

Having established the *raison d'etre* for the use of some policy measures to cure the problem of unemployment, it is now necessary to specify the instruments that are available to the government authorities for this purpose. We will consider two such instruments in this chapter: (1) monetary policy in the form of open-market operations and (2) fiscal operations in the form of deficit spending on tradables and nontradables. These policies can be applied under a regime of fixed exchange rates or when exchange rates are flexible. Policy-determined changes in the exchange rate from one fixed level to another (that is, devaluation or revaluation) represent another instrument in the hands of the government. But since it may be used for purposes other than stabilization of the domestic economy, this policy will be treated separately in the next chapter.

Fiscal operations involve the budget constraint of the government. In addition to expenditures on tradables and nontradables, the government must pay interest on its debt. As was pointed out in Chapter 3, only the debt held by the public (both domestic residents and foreigners) is relevant for this calculation. On the revenue side, the government collects taxes and sells its obligations either to the private sector or the central bank. Thus the budget constraint faced by the government is

$$\Gamma + \dot{S} + \dot{V} = G_t + G_n + rV, \qquad (4.17)$$

where Γ represents tax receipts, $\dot{S}$ and $\dot{V}$ are new issues of government securities per period of time (e.g., $\dot{S} = dS/dt$) purchased by the central bank and the private sector, respectively, G_t and G_n are expenditures (in value terms) on tradables and nontradables and rV represents interest payments to the public (r is the interest rate and V is the value of bonds held by the public). If it is now assumed that the government collects just sufficient lump-sum (that is, nondistortionary) taxes to cover interest payments, the budget constraint reduces to

$$\dot{S} + \dot{V} = G_t + G_n \tag{4.18}$$

which dictates that all new government expenditures are financed by bond issues. However, this new constraint does not imply that the interest payments and their associated tax receipts have no further impact on the economy. Since domestic residents pay $\Gamma\,(= rV)$ in taxes but receive only $r(V - V^*)$ in interest payments, with rV^* going to foreigners who hold V^* of domestic bonds, it can be seen from equation (3.64) that an ever-increasing trade balance in goods is necessary to offset the rising interest payments to foreigners. As long as foreigners are accumulating some of the bond issues engendered by the deficit spending—a condition necessary for equalization of domestic and foreign interest rates—the economy will never by able to settle down to a static equilibrium. Hence, with some reluctance, interest payments and tax receipts will be assumed not to exist, although it is sufficient to specify that they are constant and equal to each other. The alternative of stipulating that new expenditures are tax financed and that interest payments are financed by new bond issues does not alleviate the situation, since under this assumption, the government deficit is not subject to a policy decision and fiscal policy becomes a passive and weak instrument. Because, in full equilibrium, desired wealth is constant and therefore saving is reduced to zero, the standard balanced-budget multiplier is also zero. In any case, this assumption does not seriously compromise the quantitative aspects of the model as long as foreign indebtedness (V^*) is relatively small.[c]

Monetary and fiscal policies have quite different operational characteristics in the model since the former represents a one-time disturbance in the *stocks* of assets while the latter involves a one-time change in the *flow* of goods, but with a *continuing* effect on the stocks of assets caused by the financing of the government expenditures. The financing of the deficit is an important aspect of this model and requires further examination. Since bond sales to the central bank involve a combination of monetary and fiscal policies, it is assumed that $\dot{S} = 0$ and that the bond sales are absorbed by the public. Thus

---

[c]Another reason for ignoring interest payments and their associated taxes is that when measuring impact effects of policy changes, these variables will not be affected until a subsequent time period.

$$\dot{V} = G_t + G_n \qquad (4.19)$$

Because bond holdings are a component of domestic wealth, deficit financing will have continuous effects on portfolios. Taking time derivatives of equation (3.15a) with $\dot{S} = 0$ produces

$$\dot{W} = \dot{R} + \dot{V} - \dot{V}^* \qquad (4.20)$$

where W is total domestic wealth; R represents central bank holdings of international reserves; and V^* stands for foreign holdings of domestic bonds. Now

$$\dot{R} = B + \dot{V}^* \qquad (4.21)$$

which represents the balance of payments in a fixed exchange rate system: B is the trade balance; and $\dot{V}^*$ is the capital account balance per unit of time. Substituting (4.19) and (4.21) into (4.20) results in

$$\dot{W} = G_t + G_n + B \qquad (4.22)$$

This equation illustrates the sources of the growth of wealth in the SOE. If wealth is to remain constant over time, because domestic residents have achieved their desired wealth position, $\dot{W} = 0$ and

$$B = -G_t - G_n \qquad (4.23)$$

which postulates that there will be a trade deficit equal to the sum of government expenditures on tradables and nontradables to the extent that they are deficit financed.[4]

Under flexible exchange rates, $\dot{R} = 0$ in equations (4.20) and (4.21), but equation (4.22) still holds. Nevertheless, the adjustment to a new equilibrium will not be the same. Instead of adjustments in the level of international reserves held by the central bank after a change in fiscal policy, the exchange rate must adjust, engendering a sequence of events different from those if exchange rates are pegged. These differences will be highlighted in the sections, "Stabilization-Policy Effectiveness Under Fixed Exchange Rates," and "Stabilization-Policy Effectiveness Under Flexible Exchange Rates."

The impact of monetary policy, on the other hand, is relatively straightforward. In the monetary sector described in Chapter 3, only open-market operations were feasible in terms of their potential impact on the money supply. These open-market operations are depicted by the following relationship:

$$dS = -dV \qquad (4.24)$$

showing that the central bank buys (sells) government securities from the public on the open market. Expansionary monetary policy is implied if the central bank buys bonds ($dS > 0$) while contractionary monetary policy involves selling bonds ($dS < 0$).

While unemployment may be in the forefront of the economic ills facing the policy-makers, its cure is by no means the only goal to which monetary and fiscal policies are devoted. All governments whether in small or large countries desire low unemployment, little or no inflation, steady growth , balance-of-payments equilibrium, and a "favorable" trade balance. (There may be other goals that are essentially microeconomic in nature, such as an "equitable" income distribution, etc.) For a small, open economy, balance-of-payments equilibrium is achieved at any exchange rate, as was pointed out in Chapter 3, and therefore no conscious policy decision to achieve it is necessary. On the other hand, the trade balance, whether "favorable" or "unfavorable," is essentially determined by the level of government expenditures and may therefore be in conflict with other goals. But this conflict can be eliminated with an appropriate combination of policies as will be shown in the section, "Stabilization-Policy Effectiveness Under Fixed Exchange Rates." Perhaps the most serious conflict lies in the trade-off between unemployment and inflation. But to put this problem in perspective, it is worth noting that in describing the structure of the SOE in the last two chapters, as well as in the policy models of this chapter, inflation as a dynamic process is absent. There is only an equilibrium price level. Inflation in an SOE can only be generated either by a continuous increase in the world price of tradables or a continuous depreciation of the domestic currency. In order to focus on the static equilibrium properties of stabilization-policy models, these possibilities will not be considered here, but Chapter 6 will be devoted entirely to a discussion of the inflationary process in SOEs. The trade-off then in this model is between unemployment and once-and-for-all increases in the price level, still a serious conflict if these price increases provide disutility to the policy-makers. Nevertheless, this conflict can be resolved if monetary and fiscal policies are combined in an appropriate way, but only if flexible exchange rates prevail.

The Interaction of the Income and Wealth Constraints

Because fiscal and monetary policies can initiate disequilibrium in both the commodity and asset markets, the complete dichotomization of the two sets of markets is no longer a viable premise. Thus, a link between the income and wealth constraints is provided by stipulating a desired level of wealth and a wealth adjustment process. Hence,

$$\overline{W}/p = \mu y \tag{4.25}$$

and

$$E = Y - \gamma[\overline{W} - W(t-1)] \qquad (4.26)$$

where $\overline{W}$ and W represent desired and actual nominal wealth; p is the price level; E and Y are expenditures and income in nominal terms; y represents real income; and μ and γ are positive constants.[d] Equation (4.25) predicts that asset holders wish to achieve a certain level of real wealth in relation to real income. It may be argued that other factors influence the level of desired wealth. In particular, the interest rate may determine the allocation of total resources to financial wealth and nonfinancial wealth such as human capital. However, it will be assumed that the rate of return on financial assets is roughly equal to the yield on nonfinancial assets and that other influences are of minor importance in the context of a stabilization model.

Equation (4.26) represents a condition that holds only in disequilibrium. It states that, to the extent that desired wealth exceeds actual wealth in the previous period, expenditures on tradables and nontradables will fall short of income, the residual being saved, creating additions to wealth. It should be noted that as long as $\gamma < 1$, desired and actual wealth will only coincide after an infinitely long adjustment process.

The saving behavior in this model is considerably at odds with that postulated by the Keynesian consumption function where saving (additions to wealth) continues no matter what the desired level of wealth is. However, it is consistent with some of the more recent theories of consumption and saving, as, for instance, those of Milton Friedman[5] and A. K. Ando and Franco Modigliani,[6] where individuals are assumed to maximize life-time consumption subject to a life-time income constraint.

To see how the income and wealth constraints are interrelated, assume the application of a policy that increases the price level, but has no direct impact on the actual level of wealth.[e] Now, real wealth will decline below that level desired by asset holders. They will save to make up the difference, requiring that income exceeds expenditures during the process. Once desired wealth is achieved, $\overline{W} = W$ and $Y = E$. In the new full equilibrium, wealth is constant at a higher nominal level and apportioned between the two assets available to the public, money and bonds, and all income is spent on tradables and nontradables.

However, a stability condition is involved in this adjustment process. Starting with full equilibrium in period $(t - 1)$ so that $\overline{W}(t - 1) = W(t - 1)$, differentiating equation (4.26) produces

$$dE = dY - \gamma d\overline{W} \qquad (4.27)$$

and differentiating equation (4.25) gives

---

[d]Variables without a time subscript refer to the present period.

[e]Open-market operations under flexible exchange rates would be an example of this type of policy.

$$d\overline{W} = \mu dY \qquad (4.28)$$

since $Y = py$. Combining these two equations results in

$$dE = (1 - \gamma\mu)dY \qquad (4.29)$$

In this equation, $(1 - \gamma\mu)$ may be interpreted as the marginal propensity to spend, which is restricted to a value of less than one but greater than zero. Thus an increase in nominal income results in a higher level of desired wealth requiring some saving to close the gap between desired and actual wealth, but at the same time, expenditures on goods and services will also increase.

The Complete Stabilization-Policy Model of an SOE

In this section, the complete system of equations necessary to analyze the effects of a change in monetary and fiscal policies will be developed. Because R.A. Mundell found that fiscal policy was only effective if fixed exchange rates prevail while monetary policy was only operative if exchange rates are allowed to fluctuate, it is crucial that both types of exchange rate systems be considered in designing the structure of the model.[7]

In analyzing the effectiveness of stabilization policies, the major focus is on the impact of these measures on real income or output and indirectly on unemployment. But, since a change in monetary or fiscal policies may adversely affect a number of other goal variables in the system, such as the price level or the trade balance, it will be important to keep in mind the trade-offs among various goals faced by the policy-makers and to determine whether an efficient combination of policy instruments exists that allows for the simultaneous achievement of several goals.

The following notation will be used to describe the variables in the model:

p_t, p_n = domestic price of tradables and nontradables, set initially equal to one by an appropriate choice of quantity units

p_t^* = world price of tradables in a numeraire currency

π = exchange rate (that is, price of foreign currency in terms of the domestic currency), set initially equal to one

p = aggregate price level

A_t, A_n = domestic private demand for tradables and nontradables, in quantity terms

Q_t, Q_n = domestic output of tradables and nontradables, in quantity terms

G_t, G_n = government expenditures on tradables and nontradables, in value terms

E, Y = nominal level of domestic private expenditures and total national income

B = balance of trade, in value terms

y = real level of income or output

S, R = central bank holdings of government securities and international reserves ($S + R$ equals the money supply)

V = value of government bonds held by domestic and foreign residents

V^* = value of government bonds held by foreign residents only

W, $\overline{W}$ = actual and desired levels of nominal wealth of domestic residents

r, r^* = domestic and world rates of interest

The model is depicted by the following set of equations

$$p_t A_t(p_t, p_n, E) + G_t + B = p_t Q_t(p_t) \tag{4.30}$$

$$p_n A_n(p_t, p_n, E) + G_n = p_n Q_n(p_n) \tag{4.31}$$

$$E = p_t A_t + p_n A_n \tag{4.32}$$

$$Y = p_t Q_t + p_n Q_n \tag{4.33}$$

$$Y - E = G_t + G_n + B \tag{4.34}$$

$$S + R = f(Y/W, r)W \tag{4.35}$$

$$V = F(Y/W, r)W + V^* \tag{4.36}$$

$$W = S + R + V - V^* \tag{4.37}$$

$$E = Y - \gamma[\overline{W} - W(t - 1)] \tag{4.38}$$

$$W = \mu Y \tag{4.39}$$

$$\dot{y} = Y/p \tag{4.40}$$

$$p = \theta_t p_t + (1 - \theta_t)p_n \tag{4.41}$$

$$p_t = \pi p_t^* \tag{4.42}$$

$$r - r^* - \alpha[\pi - \pi(t - 1)]/\pi = 0 \tag{4.43}$$

These equations can now be discussed in some detail. Equations (4.30) and (4.31) represent equilibrium conditions in the tradable and nontradable commodity markets, respectively, both written in value terms. The $A_t(\ )$ and $A_n(\ )$ functions are homogeneous of degree zero in prices and total expenditures and are similar to those in Chapter 2. The supply functions are based on equations (4.15) and (4.16) where $\sigma = 0$. It is worth noting once more that the burden of the underemployment equilibrium is borne by these two supply functions. To ensure that they remain relevant both before and after a policy change, it is necessary to restrict the size of these policy changes so that the economy does not quite reach full employment where the supply functions of equations (4.11) and (4.12) would be appropriate. In the tradable sector, private domestic demand is augmented by government expenditures in that sector and foreign demand, as represented by the trade balance, while in the nontradable sector only government expenditures are added to private demand.

Equations (4.32) and (4.33) are definitions of private domestic expenditures and nominal national income, respectively. Equation (4.34) shows the relationship between these two variables in that $\dot{W} = Y - E$, so that an excess of income over expenditures represents saving or the accumulation of wealth while the sources of the wealth accumulation are given by equation (4.22). Equations (4.35) and (4.36) represent the equilibrium conditions in the domestic money and bond markets, in nominal terms, and are structured along similar lines as those in Chapter 3. The wealth constraint in equation (4.37) is the same as equation (3.15a) in that chapter. While equation (4.34) indicates how savings are generated, equation (4.38) stipulates why domestic residents want to save. It represents the disequilibrium link between income and expenditures discussed in the section, "The Interaction of the Income and Wealth Constraint," while equation (4.39) determines the level of desired nominal wealth also discussed above. Equation (4.40) defines the level of real income. The price level, according to equation (4.41), is composed of a weighted average (with fixed value-of-production weights) of the prices in the two sectors, ($\theta_t = p_t q_t / Y$ and $1 - \theta_t = p_n Q_n / Y$). Equation (4.42) links the domestic price of tradables to the (fixed) world price of the same goods through the exchange rate. Finally, equation (4.43) stipulates that because of perfect capital mobility, the hedged interest differential is zero. In the case of fixed exchange rates, $\pi(t) = \pi(t - 1)$ and $r = r^*$ allowing for the substitution of the world interest rate for the domestic interest rate in equations (4.35) and (4.36).

As it stands, this system of equations is overdetermined. In Chapter 3, it was pointed out that the equilibrium condition in the bond market is superfluous if the equilibrium condition in the money market is satisfied and if the wealth constraint specifies only these two assets. Thus, equation (4.36) is not a necessary component of the model. By an analogous argument, equations (4.30), (4.31) and (4.34) are not all independent of each other.[f] Thus, equation (4.31) is dropped from the model, and equilibrium in the nontradable sector is determined residually. Furthermore, equation (4.32) can itself be eliminated since E is also determined in equation (4.38). But with these eliminations, the model would now be underdetermined unless the exchange rate system is specified. This is accomplished by deleting R from the set of endogenous variables if a flexible exchange rate prevails and removing π from this set when a fixed exchange rate system is in force.

From equations (4.38) and (4.43), it is evident that the economy does not adjust instantaneously to a new equilibrium after an exogenous shock to the system. Because it was argued earlier that only the impact effects of policy changes are relevant, we are interested only in the adjustments of the endogenous variables for the arbitrary period from $(t - 1)$ to (t). For simplicity, it is assumed that adjustments to all prior shocks have ceased and that the system is in full equilibrium in period $(t - 1)$ which implies that $E(t - 1) = Y(t - 1)$ because $\overline{W}(t - 1) = W(t - 1)$ and also that, in the case of flexible exchange rates, $\pi(t - 1) = \pi(t - 2) = \ldots = \pi(t - n)$.

Although the adjustment period is arbitrary in length, it plays a crucial role in determining the impact multipliers of monetary or fiscal policy. The model contains equations that describe flows per period of time and those that involve stocks existing at some point in time. In addition, there are relationships, pertaining only to the adjustment period and not specified above, which involve both flows and changes in stocks over some period of time. In the context of comparative statics analysis, this requires that first differences of some equations from period $(t - 1)$ to (t) be taken before the model is differentiated.

Let the operator D represent the first difference in a variable such that $Dx = x(t) - x(t - 1)$ for any variable x. Applying this procedure to equation (4.37) results in

$$DW = DS + DR + DV - DV^* \qquad (4.44)$$

Now, fiscal and monetary operations—the policy variables in the system—during this period are described by

$$DV = G_t + G_n - DS \qquad (4.45)[g]$$

If open-market operations are absent, then $DS = 0$ and if deficit spending by the government is absent, then $G_t + G_n = 0$. During this same time period, the balance-of-payments relationship is depicted by

$$DR = B + DV^* \qquad (4.46)$$

---

[f]For instance, adding the first two equations and using the definitions in (4.32) and (4.33) produces $Y - E = G_t + G_n + B$ which is equation (4.34).

[g]For purposes of brevity, time subscripts referring to the present period (t) are omitted.

This can be rewritten as

$$DR = B(t - 1) + DB + DV^*$$

$$= -G_t(t - 1) - G_n(t - 1) + DB + DV^* \qquad (4.47)$$

as required by equation (4.23). Substituting (4.45) and (4.47) into (4.44) produces

$$DW = DG_t + DG_n + DB$$

which is the comparative statics equivalent of (4.22). Differentiating this equation totally with respect to current values of the variables [since variables in period $(t - 1)$ are unaffected in a comparative statics exercise beginning in (t)] results in

$$dW = dG_t + dG_n + dB \qquad (4.48)$$

While the proof of equation (4.48) assumed fixed exchange rates, it can be shown that it also holds for the case of flexible exchange rates where $DR = 0$, by definition.

Stabilization-Policy Effectiveness Under Fixed Exchange Rates

We may now begin our examination of the effectiveness of monetary and fiscal policies as stabilization instruments in a small open economy with fixed exchange rates. An analogous discussion of this topic, but with a regime of flexible exchange rates, will be taken up in the next section.

Once the exchange rate system is specified, the system of equations becomes fully determined. Thus, holding π as well as p_t^* and r^* constant (the last two variables are assumed to remain unaffected by domestic stabilization policies in the SOE), we can now differentiate the relevant equations [(4.30), (4.33) to (4.35), (4.38) to (4.41) and repeating equation (4.48)]:

$$A'_{t, p_n} dp_n + A'_{t, E} dE + dG_t + dB = 0 \qquad (4.49)$$

$$dY = (Q_n + Q'_n)dp_n \qquad (4.50)$$

$$dY - dE = dG_t + dG_n + dB \qquad (4.51)$$

$$dS + dR = f'_{Y/W} dY + (f - f'_{Y/W}Y/W)dW \qquad (4.52)$$

$$dE = dY - \gamma d\overline{W} \qquad (4.53)$$

$$d\overline{W} = \mu dY \qquad (4.54)$$

$$dy = dY - Ydp \qquad (4.55)$$

$$dp = (1 - \theta_t)dp_n \qquad (4.56)$$

$$dW = dG_t + dG_n + dB \qquad (4.57)$$

where $A'_{t, p_n} = \partial A_t/\partial p_n > 0$, on the basis that A_t and A_n are substitutes to the consumers and neither good is inferior. Also, as was argued in Chapter 3, $f - f'_{Y/W} Y/W > 0$. All partial derivatives are assumed to be constant for small changes in the variables.

This system of nine equations contains an equal number of endogenous variables (dp_n, dE, dB, dY, dR, dW, $d\overline{W}$, dy, and dp) and three policy-determined exogenous variables (dG_t, dG_n, and dS). By substitution, this system of equations can be reduced to

$$
\begin{bmatrix}
\beta_1 & A'_{t, E}(1 - \gamma\mu) & 1 & 0 \\
f'_{Y/W} Y & f'_{Y/W} & f - f'_{Y/W} Y/W & -1 \\
-Q'_n \dfrac{1}{1 - \theta_t} & 1 & 0 & 0 \\
\gamma\mu Y & \gamma\mu & -1 & 0
\end{bmatrix}
\begin{bmatrix}
dp \\
dy \\
dB \\
dR
\end{bmatrix}
$$

$$
=
\begin{bmatrix}
-dG_t \\
dS - (f - f'_{Y/W} Y/W)(dG_t + dG_n) \\
0 \\
dG_t + dG_n
\end{bmatrix}
\qquad (4.58)
$$

where $\beta_1 = A'_{t, p_n}[1/(1 - \theta_t)] + A'_{t, E}(1 - \gamma\mu)Y > 0$ as long as $1 - \gamma\mu > 0$.[h] Let Δ be the determinant of (4.58). Thus

$$\Delta = \beta_1 + Q'_n[A'_{t,E}(1 - \gamma\mu) + \gamma\mu] + \gamma\mu Y > 0$$

The Monetary- and Fiscal-Policy Multipliers

In this model, the exogenous policy variables are dG_t and dG_n for fiscal policy and dS for monetary policy. The financing of the new government expenditures is not explicitly in this set of equations, but it is implicit in equation (4.19). Also, the offsetting change in private holdings of government bonds as a result of open-market operations is not visible since equilibrium in the bond market is determined residually.

---

[h]See the discussion in the section, "The Interaction of the Income and Wealth Constraints."

The policy multipliers relevant to a fixed exchange-rate system can now be derived. They are contained in Table 4-1. The first four rows of Table 4-1 are derived directly from the solution of the system of equations (4.58), while the last row is obtained from equations (4.54) or (4.57). Other policy multipliers, not listed in the table, could be derived in a similar fashion.

Let us discuss the operation of these policies and their effects in some detail. First, consider the impact of expansionary monetary policy, which involves the central bank buying bonds from the public. This represents a one-time disruption of asset holders' portfolios. The initial impact is to lower the domestic interest rate below that level prevailing in the rest of the world, causing foreigners to sell domestic government bonds back to the residents of the SOE until the world and domestic interest rates are again equal. This capital outflow causes a balance-of-payments deficit (the trade balance remains at the level dictated by existing government expenditures), which reduces the money supply back to its original level. The commodity markets have not been influenced by this action as can be seen by the fact that neither the price level nor total real income (output) have changed. Therefore, monetary policy is ineffective as a stabilization policy instrument.

Next, consider expansionary fiscal policy in the nontradable sector.[i] An increase in government demand in the nontradable sector creates excess demand in that sector at the prevailing price. Thus p_n will rise. This causes an expansion of output at the expense of unemployment (as opposed to reduced output of tradables) and thus an unambiguous increase in total output or real income. At the same time, the increased government expenditures involve a larger deficit and the bonds issued to cover this deficit will be taken up by domestic residents to the extent that they desire a higher level of nominal wealth, the residual (if any) being absorbed by foreign asset portfolios. There will, in addition, be a one-time balance-of-payments surplus, since with a higher price level and increased real income, domestic residents will want to hold larger nominal money balances. If desired wealth had not increased, the trade balance would have fallen by the extent of the increase in government expenditures, as would be the case if G_t were increased. But, since $d\overline{W} = \gamma dW > 0$, equation (4.48) dictates that the decline in the trade balance will be less than the increase in G_n.

These results are in complete harmony with those originally derived by Mundell.[j] He, as well as Argy and Porter,[8] found that, under fixed exchange rates, monetary policy is unable to increase aggregate demand in the economy and therefore it becomes an inoperative stabilization-policy instrument. On the other hand, fiscal policy is effective under these cir-

[i]Fiscal policy in the tradable sector only influences the trade balance and is therefore of little interest by itself.

[j]In Appendix 4A of this chapter, Mundell's model is presented to facilitate comparisons with the results in this and the next section.

Table 4-1
Monetary- and Fiscal-Policy Multipliers Under Fixed Exchange Rates

Variable Affected by Policy	Monetary Policy $dS > 0$	Fiscal Policy	
		$dG_t > 0$	$dG_n > 0$
dy	0	0	$\dfrac{1}{\Delta} Q'_n \dfrac{1}{1 - \theta_t} > 0$
dp	0	0	$\dfrac{1}{\Delta} > 0$
dR	-1	0	$\dfrac{1}{\Delta}\left[\left(Q'_n \dfrac{1}{1 - \theta_t} + Y \right) (f'_{Y/W} + \right.$ $\left. \gamma\mu(f - f'_{Y/W}Y/W)) \right] > 0$
dB	0	-1	$-1 < \dfrac{1}{\Delta}\left[-\beta_1 - Q'_n \dfrac{1}{1 - \theta_t} A'_{t,E} \right.$ $\left. (1 - \gamma\mu) \right] < 0$
$d\overline{W} = \gamma dW$	0	0	$\dfrac{\mu}{\Delta}\left[Q'_n \dfrac{1}{1 - \theta_t} + Y \right] > 0$

cumstances. It should be pointed out that both Mundell and Argy and Porter assume an infinitely elastic supply of goods at the prevailing price (that is, output is completely demand determined) and thus the price level is held constant. This particular result could be derived from the present analysis by assuming $Q'_n \to \infty$ and dropping the price arguments in the demand functions.

Policy Combinations to Achieve a Number of Economic Goals

The policy-makers in an SOE may be in a situation where a change in aggregate demand and total output is only one of their goals. For instance, they may want to expand output without an increase in the price level. From an inspection of the multipliers in Table 4-1, it can be seen that this combination of goals is impossible to achieve.[k] In a sense, the economy has only one effective policy (that is, expenditure policy in the nontradable sector) and two divergent goals. Thus one goal must be sacrificed.

---

[k]In the next section, it will be shown that such a combination is possible with flexible exchange rates.

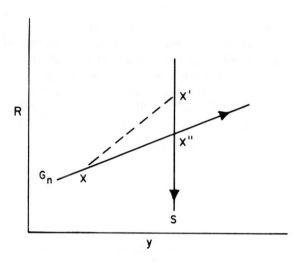

Figure 4-1. Policy Combination to Achieve Higher Income and Reserves

However, other combinations of goals can be envisaged. For instance, policy-makers may want increased output and a higher level of reserves (that is, a temporary balance-of-payments surplus). From the last column in Table 4-1, it can be seen that expansionary fiscal policy in the nontradable sector will move the economy in the right direction with respect to both goals. Figure 4-1 depicts the situation graphically. With the two goal variables on the axes, a positively sloped line can be drawn that indicates the effect of fiscal policy in the nontradable sector. The slope of this line is

$$\left(\frac{dR}{dy} \right)_{G_n} = \frac{\left(\dfrac{1}{1 - \theta_t} Q'_n + Y \right) [f'_{Y/W} + \gamma\mu(f - f'_{Y/W} Y/W)]}{\dfrac{1}{1 - \theta_t} Q'_n} \tag{4.59}$$

$$> 0$$

The arrow on the G_n line indicates the direction for expansionary policy. Assume that the economy is at a point such as X and that policy-makers want to reach another point such as X'. In order to achieve this position, the authorities must use expansionary fiscal policy that moves the economy to X'' and contractionary monetary policy to move the economy from X'' to X'. The slope of the S line is

$$\left(\frac{dR}{dy} \right)_S = \frac{-1}{0} \to -\infty \tag{4.60}$$

and thus monetary policy only affects the level of reserves.

Another example of combined goals would be the aim of increased aggregate demand without a larger deficit in the trade balance. Here, the optimal policy combination would be an increase in government demand for nontradables coupled with a decrease in the demand for tradables. The first policy increases aggregate demand and creates a larger deficit in the trade balance while the second policy improves the trade balance without deleterious effects on total output.

Stabilization-Policy Effectiveness Under Flexible Exchange Rates

Under a regime of flexible exchange rates, the model has several characteristics that are different from those when fixed exchange rates prevail. In the first place, changes in the price of tradables are determined by changes in the exchange rate, if the world price of tradables is constant. Second, since official intervention in the foreign exchange market is precluded by the "rules of the game," it is assumed that the central bank holds no international reserves; thus, changes in the money supply are determined solely by open-market operations which implies that the money supply is exogenous. Finally, the domestic interest rate is no longer always equal to the world interest rate; it is now determined by both the world interest rate and the premium or discount on forward foreign exchange contracts, since perfect capital mobility now implies an equalization of hedged yields.[1]

In addition to the equations used for the fixed exchange rate model, equations (4.42) and (4.43) are now relevant. Holding R, p_t^*, and r^* constant, these equations are now totally differentiated:

$$(A_t + A'_{t, p_t} - Q_t - Q'_t)dp_t + A'_{t, p_n} dp_n$$
$$+ A'_{t,E} dE + dG_t + dB = 0 \qquad (4.61)$$

$$dY = (Q_t + Q'_t)dp_t + (Q_n + Q'_n)dp_n \qquad (4.62)$$

$$dY - dE = dG_t + dG_n + dB \qquad (4.63)$$

$$dS = f'_{Y/W} dY + (f - f'_{Y/W}Y/W)dW + f'_r W \, dr \qquad (4.64)$$

$$dE = dY - \gamma d\overline{W} \qquad (4.65)$$

$$d\overline{W} = \mu dY \qquad (4.66)$$

$$dy = dY - Ydp \qquad (4.67)$$

---

[1]This point was discussed in some detail in the section, "The Forward Market and Flexible Exchange Rates," Chapter 3.

$$dp = \theta_t dp_t + (1 - \theta_t)dp_n \qquad (4.68)$$

$$dr - \alpha\pi(t - 1)d\pi = 0 \qquad (4.69)$$

$$dp_t = d\pi \qquad (4.70)$$

$$dW = dG_t + dG_n + dB \qquad (4.71)$$

The endogenous variables in this eleven-equation model are: dp_t, dp_n, dE, dB, dY, dW, $d\overline{W}$, dr, dy, dp, and $d\pi$; the exogenous variables are dG_t, dG_n, and dS. By a process of substitution, this system can be reduced to four equations written in matrix form as

$$
\begin{bmatrix}
\beta_2 & \beta_3 & A'_{t,E}(1 - \gamma\mu) & 1 \\
\beta_4 & f'_{Y/W}Q_n & f'_{Y/W} & f - f'_{Y/W} \, Y/W \\
-Q'_t & -Q'_n & 1 & 0 \\
\gamma\mu Q_t & \gamma\mu Q_n & \gamma\mu & -1
\end{bmatrix}
\begin{bmatrix}
d\pi \\
dp_n \\
dy \\
dB
\end{bmatrix}
$$

$$
=
\begin{bmatrix}
-dG_t \\
dS - (f - f'_{Y/W}Y/W)(dG_t + dG_n) \\
0 \\
dG_t + dG_n
\end{bmatrix}
\qquad (4.72)
$$

where

$$\beta_2 = A_t + A'_{t,p_t} - Q_t - Q'_t + A'_{t,E}(1 - 1\,\gamma\mu)Q_t$$

$$= A_t(1 + \eta_{A_t,p_t}) - Q_t[1 - A'_{t,E}(1 - \gamma\mu)] - Q'_t < 0$$

as long as $\eta_{A_t,p_t} \le -1$, where η refers to the elasticity with respect to the subscripted variables. (A profit-maximizing equilibrium would require this condition as long as marginal cost is positive.) Also,

$$\beta_3 = A'_{t,p_n} + A'_{t,E}(1 - \gamma\mu)Q_n > 0$$

unambiguously, while

$$\beta_4 = f'_{Y/W}Q_t + f'_r W\alpha\pi(t - 1) > 0$$

as long as $\alpha < 0$. This means that speculators' expectations are inelastic which is the most reasonable assumption if the foreign exchange market is to be stable dynamically. (There are positive values of α which are consistent with $\beta_4 > 0$, but it will be assumed henceforth that $\alpha \le 0$.)

Table 4-2
Monetary- and Fiscal-Policy Multipliers Under Flexible Exchange Rates

Variable Affected by Policy	Monetary Policy $dS > 0$
dy	$\dfrac{1}{\Delta'}\left[Q'_t(\gamma\mu Q_n + \beta_3) + Q'_n\left\{Q_t(1 - \gamma\mu)(1 - A'_{t,E}) + Q'_t\right.\right.$ $\left.\left. - A_t(1 + \eta_{A_t, p_t})\right\}\right] > 0$
$d\pi = dp_t$	$\dfrac{1}{\Delta'}\left[\gamma\mu(Q_t + Q'_t) + \beta_3 + Q'_n A'_{t,E}(1 - \gamma\mu)\right] > 0$
dp_n	$\dfrac{1}{\Delta'}\left[(Q_t + Q'_t)(1 - \gamma\mu)(1 - A'_{t,E})\right.$ $\left. - A_t(1 + \eta_{A_t, p_t})\right] > 0$
dp	$\theta_t\dfrac{dp_t}{dS} + (1 - \theta_t)\dfrac{dp_n}{dS} > 0$
dB	$\mu\left(\dfrac{dy}{dS} + Y\dfrac{dp}{dS}\right) > 0$
dr	$\alpha\pi(t - 1)\dfrac{d\pi}{dS} < 0$
$d\overline{W} = \gamma dW$	$\mu\left(\dfrac{dy}{dS} + Y\dfrac{dp}{dS}\right) > 0$

The Monetary- and Fiscal-Policy Multipliers

Denoting Δ' as the determinant of (4.72), it can be shown that $\Delta' > 0$. Policy multipliers analogous to those for fixed exchange rates are indicated in Table 4-2. In this table, η_{Q_t} and η_{Q_n} are the supply elasticities of tradables and nontradables. For brevity,

$$\beta_5 = \gamma\mu(f - f'_{Y/W}Y/W) + f'_{Y/W} > 0$$

In evaluating the expressions for the multipliers it is assumed that $\eta_{A_t, p_t} \leq -1$ and that $\alpha < 0$.

The monetary-policy multipliers are consistent with those derived by Mundell, except, of course, that he assumed a constant price level. Expansionary monetary policy initially creates excess domestic demand for bonds and excess supply of money. This has a tendency to raise the price of bonds or lower their yield. Assuming that foreign and domestic interest rates were equal in the original equilibrium (implying a zero premium on forward contracts), foreigners will want to rid themselves of domestic

Fiscal Policy

$dG_t > 0$	$dG_n > 0$
0	$\dfrac{1}{\Delta'}[Q_t Q_n \beta_5(\eta_{Q_n} - \eta_{Q_t}) + Q_n' f_r' W\alpha\pi(t-1)] = ?$
0	$-\dfrac{1}{\Delta'}[\beta_5(Q_n + Q_n')] < 0$
0	$\dfrac{1}{\Delta'}[\gamma\mu(f - f_{Y/W}' Y/W)(Q_t + Q_t') + \beta_4 + f_{Y/W}'Q_t'] > 0$
0	$\dfrac{1}{\Delta'}\left[\dfrac{Q_t Q_n}{Y}\beta_5(\eta_{Q_t} - \eta_{Q_n}) + (1 - \theta_t)f_r' W\alpha\pi(t-1)\right] = ?$
-1	$-\left[\beta_2\dfrac{dp_t}{dG_n} + A_{t,p_n}'\dfrac{dp_n}{dG_n} + A_{t,E}'\dfrac{dE}{dY}\dfrac{dY}{dG_n}\right] < 0$
0	$\alpha\pi(t-1)\dfrac{d\pi}{dG_n} > 0$
0	$\dfrac{1}{\Delta'}[\mu f_r' W\alpha\pi(t-1)(Q_n + Q_n')] > 0$

bonds. This will cause a depreciation of the domestic currency ($d\pi > 0$). Speculators will adjust their expectations of future rates, and if $\alpha < 0$, the forward exchange rate will decline. So that the hedged yield on domestic bonds equals the unchanged world interest rate in the new temporary equilibrium, the domestic interest rate will be lower than originally as dictated by equation (4.69). Since a depreciation of the domestic currency is translated directly into an equivalent increase in the domestic price of tradables, as required by equation (4.70), output of tradables will increase. At the same time, consumers will shift from tradables to nontradables as relative prices have shifted in favor of the latter, causing the price in that sector to increase as well and stimulating further output of nontradables. As a result, both real income and the price level have risen. After the initial effects of the expansion of the money supply, nominal wealth will be higher because income has risen. In summary, expansionary monetary policy is an effective stabilization-policy instrument if policy-makers have a lower level of unemployment as their goal. Conversely, contractionary policy is effective if a lower price level is the policy-maker's aim.

The fiscal-policy multipliers in Table 4-2, on the other hand, do not coincide with Mundell's prediction that fiscal policy is inoperative as a stabilization-policy instrument when exchange rates are flexible.[9] Inspecting the multipliers in the last column of Table 4-2, which deal with the effects of fiscal policy in the nontradable sector, we see that this policy measure does affect the level of income and prices as long as $\eta_{Q_t} \neq \eta_{Q_n}$ and $\alpha \neq 0$. By way of contrast, Mundell's model contained only one homogenous commodity and its output could be expanded without increases in prices as well as the assumption that perfect capital mobility resulted in the equalization of the unhedged interest rates. If these conditions are imposed on the multipliers in Table 4-2, his original conclusions are reestablished. But his assumption of infinitely elastic supply of output seems to be relevant only to an economy suffering from a severe case of depression and not to the contemporary scene, while his capital-mobility assumption denies that investors take into account exchange rate risks when deciding on their optimum portfolios.

Because of the indeterminacies in the multipliers for fiscal policy in the nontradable sector, it is difficult to describe the entire sequence of events which follow in the train of a one-time change in that policy, but some highlights can be indicated. As was the case with fixed exchange rates, the increased government expenditures create excess demand in the nontradable sector, causing output to rise because of the higher price that is necessary to clear the market. With a higher level of prices and income, domestic residents will want to accumulate money balances and wealth in general. While they are unable to increase their holdings of domestic money, they can purchase bonds from foreigners, which causes an appreciation of the domestic currency (that is, $d\pi < 0$).[m]

With the lower exchange rate, the domestic price of tradables must fall, causing a decline in output in that sector and, in general, reversing the above-mentioned expansionary effects. Whether real income or the price level will be higher or lower than in the original equilibrium depends to a large extent on the relative size of the two supply elasticities. At the same time as the domestic currency is appreciating, speculators will cause the forward rate to rise, resulting in a higher domestic interest rate in order that the hedged yield on domestic bonds is again equal to the constant world interest rate.

Since the supply of money remains unchanged, equilibrium in the money market requires adjustments in Y and/or W to offset the rise in the interest rate. It can be shown that both Y and W increase, but not in the

---

[m]In fact, they obtain the bonds directly from the deficit financing. But in order to maintain balance-of-payments equilibrium at the *existing* exchange rate, it is necessary that all the new bonds be acquired by foreigners. Then, when domestic residents buy some of the bonds "back," the domestic currency appreciates.

same proportion.[n] This larger amount of nominal wealth is composed of an unchanged amount of money and higher bond holdings, a situation which is consistent with the higher interest rate.

For greater clarity, the effect of deficit financing in the nontradable sector on the trade balance is expressed in terms of other multipliers satisfying equation (4.61). This expression shows that there is an unambiguous decline in the trade balance.

The important conclusion from this discussion is that while fiscal policy may be an effective stabilization-policy instrument, it can also be perverse in its effects compared with the traditional results. This means that policy-makers must be aware of the structure of the economy in order to prevent undesirable effects of fiscal-policy action. For instance, assume that the relationship among the various parameters is such that $dy/dG_n < 0$. In this case, *expansionary* fiscal policy involves a *reduction* in government expenditures in the nontradable sector. It may be argued that because of the possible perverse reaction of the economy to a change in fiscal policy, the authorities in an SOE should concentrate on monetary policy as a stabilization instrument. But there is a large pay-off to the policy-makers if they can eliminate the indeterminacies in the fiscal-policy multipliers by having at their disposal some estimates of the parameters involved, since policy combinations will then be possible that allow for the simultaneous achievement of two or more goals.[o]

Combinations of Goals and Policies Under Flexible Exchange Rates

In this section, I concentrate on the twin goals of expanding output to reduce unemployment while at the same time attempting to avoid increases in the price level.[p] Because of the large number of specific policy combinations necessary to achieve these results—due to the indeterminacies in the fiscal-policy multipliers—only two extreme cases will be considered. In Case I, it is assumed that speculators' expectations are such that $\alpha = 0$. At the same time, the two supply elasticities are assumed to be positive but different in size. In Case II, the procedure is reversed; the supply elasticities are equal in size while speculators' expectations are inelastic (that is, $\alpha < 0$). Case I coincides with the analysis by M. F. J. Prachowny[10] while Case II resembles the model postulated by Argy and Porter.[11]

[n]To determine that $dY > 0$, equation (4.67) is solved. Then, since $d\overline{W} = \mu dY$ and $d\overline{W} = \gamma dW$, it can be seen that $dW > 0$. If $\alpha = 0$, then Y and W would remain constant and any increase (decrease) in real income is offset by a decrease (increase) in the price level.

[o]A method of obtaining this information is discussed in Appendix 4B of this chapter.

[p]Other goal cominations are possible, but they are considered to be of less interest.

Case I. From the multipliers in Table 4-2, we know that expansionary monetary policy will cause an increase in real income as well as a higher price level. On the other hand, the fiscal-policy multipliers become

$$\frac{dy}{dG_n} = \frac{1}{\Delta'} \left[Q_t Q_n \beta_5 (\eta_{Q_n} - \eta_{Q_t}) \right] \tag{4.73}$$

$$\frac{dp}{dG_n} = -\frac{1}{\Delta'} \left[\frac{Q_t Q_n}{Y} \beta_5 (\eta_{Q_n} - \eta_{Q_t}) \right] \tag{4.74}$$

Thus, if $\eta_{Q_n} > \eta_{Q_t}$, increased government expenditures in the nontradable sector will increase total output as well as reducing the price level. If, on the other hand, $\eta_{Q_n} < \eta_{Q_t}$, then the reverse results will obtain.

The effects of these two policy measures can be shown in Figure 4-2. In this diagram, with the two goal variables on the axes, the line denoted by S shows the effects of monetary policy on the two goals, while G_n indicates the effects of fiscal policy in the nontradable sector. From any point such as X expansionary monetary policy will move the economy up and to the right in the direction of the arrow on line S.[q] On the other hand, expansionary fiscal policy will move the economy down and to the right if $\eta_{Q_n} > \eta_{Q_t}$ and up to the left if $\eta_{Q_n} < \eta_{Q_t}$.[r]

Assume that the economy is at X where unemployed resources exist and the aim is to move towards X' where full employment prevails. If $\eta_{Q_n} > \eta_{Q_t}$, a combination of expansionary monetary policy and expansionary fiscal policy will achieve this result without increasing the price level.[s] The reason for this fortunate result is that the two policies cancel each other out in their effect on the exchange rate (that is, the price of tradables) and the price of nontradables, but not with respect to their effects on total output. If $\eta_{Q_n} < \eta_{Q_t}$, then contractionary fiscal policy and expansionary monetary policy will give rise to the same result.

Case II. In the situation depicted in Case II, increases in prices are still necessary to obtain larger outputs of tradables or nontradables, but the response in the two sectors is assumed to be equal. Thus, $\eta_{Q_n} = \eta_{Q_t} > 0$. At the same time, speculators' expectations are inelastic ($\alpha < 0$). The fiscal-policy multipliers are now

$$\frac{dy}{dG_n} = \frac{1}{\Delta'} \left[Q'_n f'_r W \alpha \pi (t - 1) \right] > 0 \tag{4.75}$$

$$\frac{dp}{dG_n} = \frac{1}{\Delta'} \left[(1 - \theta_t) f'_r W \alpha \pi (t - 1) \right] > 0 \tag{4.76}$$

---

[q] By dividing dy/dS into dp/dS, it can be seen that $(dp/dy)_S > 0$.

[r] The slope of G_n is $(dp/dy)_{G_n} = -1/Y < 0$.

[s] These policies may be combined by financing the deficit through sales of bonds to the central bank.

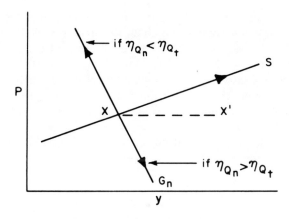

Figure 4-2. Policy Combinations to Achieve Higher Income with a Constant Price Level, Assuming $\alpha = 0$

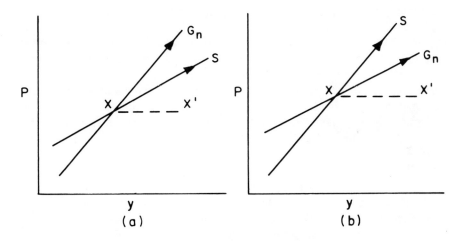

Figure 4-3. Policy Combinations to Achieve Higher Income with a Constant Price Level, Assuming $\eta_{Q_n} = \eta_{Q_t}$

Therefore, $(dp/dy)_{G_n} - (1 - \theta_t)/Q'_n > 0$. The slope of the monetary-policy line is also positive as in Case I, but in the absence of estimates of the parameters of the system, the slope of the fiscal-policy line may be steeper or flatter than the monetary-policy line. Both cases are considered in Figure 4-3. In part (a) of Figure 4-3, to move from X to X', expansionary monetary policy coupled with contractionary fiscal policy is required, while in part (b), the opposite combination is called for. This situation represents a difficult dilemma for the policy-makers, that can only be resolved by having some knowledge about the structure of the particular SOE. This same conundrum applies with equal force to Case I. It remains for the authorities in each SOE to decide whether it is worth the effort to obtain the necessary information and whether, once obtained, it is sufficiently reliable to make these important policy decisions. In view of the added degree of freedom gained by having an effective fiscal policy as well as monetary policy, it seems only reasonable to place the burden of proof on those who would argue that fiscal policy in conjunction with flexible exchange rates is either ineffective or unpredictable.

Conclusions

Under fixed exchange rates, the only policy instrument that affected income and prices was expenditure policy in the nontradable sector. In this situation, it is impossible to expand income without increasing the price level as well. But, a regime of flexible exchange rates and a minimal knowledge about the structure of the SOE in question allows for the combination of monetary and fiscal policies to generate full employment at a constant price level.

In Mundell's model, the assumption of smallness together with perfect capital mobility implied that an economy with these characteristics is essentially a price-taker in the capital account of its balance of payments and rendered certain policy instruments ineffective depending on the exchange rate system adopted by the country. By extending the assumption of smallness together with perfect goods mobility to the current account, the SOE also becomes a price-taker in the world market for tradables. While this extension may appear to increase the constraints on policy effectiveness even further, it has been shown that the opposite is true when flexible exchange rates are allowed to operate. The role of the exchange rate in determining the domestic price level and the effect of monetary and fiscal policies on the exchange rate have led to the conclusion that the trade-off between *temporary* inflation and unemployment is much less serious for an SOE than for a large or closed economy where the Phillips curve is still considered an unfortunate fact of life.

The urge to translate these conclusions into practical policy prescriptions, however, must be resisted. One should be particularly uncomfortable about investigating the role of stabilization policy in a static context when in fact policy-makers are confronted with problems of stabilization, *persistent* inflation and growth, simultaneously. While growth *per se* will receive little attention in this study, inflation as a continuing phenomenon will be discussed in Chapter 6, which will help to put the present discussion in even better perspective.

Notes

1. R. A. Mundell, "Capital Mobility and Stabilization Policy Under Fixed and Flexible Exchange Rates," *Canadian Journal of Economics and Political Science* 29 (1963): 475-85; ——, "A Reply: Capital Mobility and Size," *Canadian Journal of Economics and Political Science* 30 (1964): 421-31.

2. The guidelines for stabilization policy in a growing economy is discussed Niehans. In this context, he states, "For the time being it seems to be an illusion to believe that there are hard and fast rules about the optimal combination of monetary and fiscal policies in an open economy independent of any specific information about the economy in question." Jurg Niehans, "Monetary and Fiscal Policies in Open Economies: An Optimizing Approach," *Journal of Political Economy* 76 (1968): 905.

3. This seems to be the "modern" approach to the justification of an underemployment equilibrium. Henderson and Sargent, for instance, assume "that the money wage is rigid at any moment, the kind of assumption that is necessary to make in order to build a model in which unemployment is possible, and in which it is interesting to investigate the short-run effects on employment and output of alternative monetary and fiscal policies. The money wage rate might well respond to the imposition of disturbances on the economy; our assumption permits such adjustments to occur over time, but rules out any instantaneous adjustment in money wages." D. W. Henderson and T. J. Sargent, "Monetary and Fiscal Policy in a Two-Sector Aggregative Model," *American Economic Review* 63 (1973): 345.

4. Whitman makes this explicit in her discussion of fiscal policy. She states, " . . . an increase in deficit spending will increase the trade deficit by an equal amount . . . a deficit which is financed by the transfer of excess financial assets to foreigners." M. v. N. Whitman, *Policies for Internal and External Balance*, Special Papers in International Economics, no. 9, Princeton, N.J., Princeton University, 1970, p. 26.

5. Milton Friedman, *A Theory of the Consumption Function*, NBER study no. 63, Princeton, N.J., Princeton University Press, 1957.

6. A. K. Ando and Franco Modigliani, "The 'Life-Cycle' Hypothesis of Saving: Aggregate Implications and Tests," *American Economic Review* 53 (1963): 55-84.

7. Mundell, "Capital Mobility and Stabilization Policy"; "Capital Mobility and Size."

8. Victor Argy and M. G. Porter, "The Forward Exchange Market and the Effects of Domestic and External Disturbances Under Alternative Exchange Rate Systems," *International Monetary Fund Staff Papers* 19 (1972):503-32.

9. It is indeed true that government demand in the tradable sector has no influence on income or prices, but Mundell stipulated that only expenditures on "home goods" were to be considered. Mundell, "Capital Mobility and Stabilization Policy," p. 476.

10. M. F. J. Prachowny, "The Effectiveness of Stabilization Policy in a Small Open Economy," *Weltwirtschaftliches Archiv* 109 (1973):214-31.

11. Argy and Porter, "The Forward Exchange Market."

Appendix 4A
Mundell's Model of
Stabilization Policy
Effectiveness

R. A. Mundell has attempted to provide a rigorous proof of the proposition that for a small open economy facing perfect capital mobility, only fiscal policy is effective as a stabilization-policy instrument under fixed exchange rates, while monetary policy alone is effective if flexible exchange rates prevail.[1] The basic structure of his model is an *IS-LM* framework for two interdependent countries. The purpose of the two-country model is "to generalize the results by taking into account repercussion effects and altering the assumption that the country pursuing the policy is small. The primary complication this involves is that world interest rates may no longer be taken as given."[2] But since I am prepared to take for granted that the home country is small, the *IS-LM* structure of the second country (that is, the rest of the world) is in fact given. Because repercussions from the world economy to the SOE are the only ones in existence, the model can be truncated to the *IS-LM* structure of the home country.

In describing Mundell's model, insofar as is possible, I use the notation of this chapter. Let

y = real income (also nominal income since the price level is constant)

I = investment

s = saving

G = government expenditures

B = trade balance

S = domestic assets of the central bank (that is, government securities)

R = international reserves held by the central bank

r^* = world interest rate (equal to the domestic interest rate)

π = foreign exchange rate (price of the foreign currency in terms of the domestic currency, initially equal to one)

The structure of the model is as follows:

$$I(r^*) + G - s(y) + B(y, \pi) = 0 \qquad (4A.1)$$

$$S + R = f(y, r^*) \qquad (4A.2)$$

Equation (4A.1) is the algebraic analogue of the *IS* curve showing the equilibrium condition in the goods markets. Equation (4A.2) relates to the *LM* curve, depicting the equilibrium condition in the money market.

Most of the differences between the structure of Mundell's model and that used in this chapter have been discussed previously. Since the conclusions about policy effectiveness are identical except for the case of fiscal policy under flexible exchange rates, many of these differences are not crucial. Nevertheless, it is worth noting once more the reasons for this exception. In Mundell's model, a change in the exchange rate does not influence domestic prices nor the domestic interest rate. Once these links are broken, it is impossible to obtain a differential response to price changes in the tradable and nontradable sectors, nor can hedged foreign investments create a temporary divergence between the domestic and world interest rates.

Holding only r^* constant, equations (4A.1) and (4A.2) can be differentiated to yield

$$dG - s'dy + B'_y dy + B'_\pi d\pi = 0 \tag{4A.3}$$

$$dS + dR = f'_y dy \tag{4A.4}$$

where $s' > 0$, $B'_y < 0$, $B'_\pi > 0$ and $f'_y > 0$. These two equations contain three endogenous variables (dy, $d\pi$ and dR) and two exogenous policy variables (dG and dS). To make the system determinate, we must specify the exchange rate system in existence. Under fixed exchange rates, $d\pi = 0$, while under flexible rates, $dR = 0$.

Fixed Exchange Rates

The model now becomes

$$\begin{bmatrix} (B'_y - s') & 0 \\ f'_y & -1 \end{bmatrix} \begin{bmatrix} dy \\ dR \end{bmatrix} = \begin{bmatrix} -dG \\ dS \end{bmatrix} \tag{4A.5}$$

Thus,

$$\frac{dy}{dG} = - \frac{1}{B'_y - s'} > 0 \quad \text{(fiscal-policy multiplier)}$$

$$\frac{dy}{dS} = 0 \quad \text{(monetary-policy multiplier)}$$

In Mundell's words, the fiscal-policy effects are as follows:

The increased spending has a multiplier effect upon income, increasing saving, taxes, and imports. Taxes [subsumed under saving] increase by less than the increase in government spending, so the government supplies securities at a rate equal to the budget deficit, whereas the private sector absorbs securities at a rate equal to the increase in saving.[3]

Monetary-policy effects, on the other hand, he explains as follows:

A central bank purchase of securities creates excess reserves and puts downward pressure on the interest rate. But a fall in the interest rate is prevented by a capital outflow, and this worsens the balance of payments. To prevent the exchange rate from [rising], the central bank intervenes in the market, selling foreign exchange and buying domestic money. The process continues until the accumulated foreign exchange deficit is equal to the open market purchase and the money supply is restored to its original level.[4]

Flexible Exchange Rates

With this system, the model is depicted by

$$\begin{bmatrix} (B'_y - s') & B'_\pi \\ f'_y & 0 \end{bmatrix} \begin{bmatrix} dy \\ d\pi \end{bmatrix} = \begin{bmatrix} -dG \\ dS \end{bmatrix} \qquad (4A.6)$$

Therefore,

$$\frac{dy}{dG} = 0 \quad \text{(fiscal-policy multiplier)}$$

$$\frac{dy}{dS} = \frac{1}{f'_y} > 0 \quad \text{(monetary-policy multiplier)}$$

Mundell's description of the fiscal-policy effects under flexible exchange rates is, in his own words:

The increased spending creates an excess demand for goods and tends to raise income. But this would increase the demand for money, raise interest rates, attract a capital inflow, and [lower] the exchange rate, which in turn would have a depressing effect on income. In fact, therefore, the negative effect on income of [the domestic currency] appreciation has to offset exactly the positive multiplier effect on income of the original increase in government spending.[5]

Expansionary monetary policy is effective under these circumstances. Mundell states:

. . . an open market purchase . . . results in an increase in bank reserves, a multiple expansion of money and credit, and downward pressure on the rate of interest. But the interest rate is prevented from falling by an outflow of capital, which causes a deficit in the balance of payments, and a depreciation of the [domestic currency]. In turn, [this] improves the balance of trade and stimulates, by the multiplier process, income and employment.[6]

Notes

1. R. A. Mundell, "A Reply: Capital Mobility and Size," *Canadian Journal of Economics and Political Science* 30 (1964): 421-31, reprinted with minor changes in his *International Economics*, New York, the Macmillan Company, 1968, pp. 262-71.

2. Mundell, *International Economics*, pp. 262-3.

3. R. A. Mundell, "Capital Mobility and Stabilization Policy Under Fixed and Flexible Exchange Rates," *Canadian Journal of Economics and Political Science* 29 (1963): 479.

4. Ibid.

5. Ibid., p. 478.

6. Ibid., p. 477.

Appendix 4B
A Suggested Method of Resolving the Indeterminacy of the Policy Multipliers

The most important conclusion to be drawn from the analysis in Chapter 4 is that an economy operating under flexible exchange rates may be able to move towards full employment while at the same time maintaining a constant price level by applying a judicious combination of monetary and fiscal policies. The only difficulty with this prescription is that policy-makers are unable to determine the appropriate direction in which to move the policy instruments because the signs of the fiscal-policy multipliers are indeterminate. The only way to resolve this dilemma is for the authorities to obtain some reliable quantitative information concerning the structural parameters applicable to their particular economy.

One way of obtaining this information is to estimate the parameters of the structure of an SOE as described by equations (4.30) to (4.43) and then to calculate the numerical values of the multipliers in Table 4-2. With this information, the slope of the policy lines in Figures 4-2 and 4-3 could be derived and the policy prescriptions would become evident. However, this procedure is not only cumbersome but, given the scope of data availability, it may be treacherous as well. The chief stumbling block is the lack of price and quantity data for tradables and nontradables. Many arbitrary decisions would have to be made to determine to which category the output of each industry should be assigned. Theoretically, if an industry produces a homogeneous commodity that is partly sold in world markets or that competes in domestic markets with goods produced abroad, then this industry should be labelled a tradable industry. Other industries, producing goods that face no competition in world markets, should have their output included under nontradables. Empirically, this distinction is extremely difficult to draw.

The purpose of this appendix is to suggest a simpler method of estimating the policy multipliers than that discussed above. No estimates for a particular economy will be provided since the main thrust of the study is theoretical exploration rather than empirical verification, but it is important to put the theoretical framework in a form which is testable.

The proposed method of estimating the multipliers involves a number of reduced-form equations, a procedure that eliminates the need for much of the unavailable data as well as reduces the number of equations that have to be estimated. The policy multipliers for both fixed and flexible exchange rates will be discussed. Although there are no ambiguities in the signs of the policy multipliers in the former case, it may still be of some interest to have a quantitative estimate of the effects of expansionary fiscal policy on both income and prices to give the authorities some idea of the trade-off involved. (It will be remembered that monetary policy had no effect on either variable when the exchange rate is fixed.)

To obtain the reduced-form equations involves solving the system of equations (4.30) to (4.43), which means that the values of the endogenous variables are determined by the structural parameters of the system and the values of the exogenous variables. There are 11 endogenous variables in the system: $p_t, p_n, E, B, Y, W, \overline{W}, y, p, r$, and either R (under fixed exchange rates) or π (under flexible exchange rates). As discussed previously, equations (4.31), (4.32) and (4.36) are redundant, leaving 11 independent equations and resulting in a unique solution for each of the endogenous variables. The exogenous variables are $G_t, G_n, S, p_t^*, r^*, W(t-1)$, and $\pi(t-1)$. The first three of these are policy variables: G_t and G_n represent deficit spending by the government on tradables and nontradables, respectively, while changes in S are dictated by open-market operations by the central bank. On the other hand, p_t^* and r^* are determined in world markets, while $W(t-1)$ and $\pi(t-1)$ are predetermined.

The Reduced-Form Equations Under Fixed Exchange Rates

The endogenous variables of special interest are the price level and real income and therefore they will receive concentrated attention at the expense of the other variables in the system. Assuming that the relationship between the endogenous and exogenous variables is linear, the reduced-form equations can be written as follows:

$$p = b_0 + b_1 G_t + b_2 G_n + b_3 S + b_4 p_t^* + b_5 r^*$$

$$+ b_6 W(t-1) + b_7 \pi(t-1) \tag{4B.1}$$

$$y = b_8 + b_9 G_t + b_{10} G_n + b_{11} S + b_{12} p_t^* + b_{13} r^*$$

$$+ b_{14} W(t-1) + b_{15} \pi(t-1) \tag{4B.2}$$

However, because of our knowledge of the theoretical structure, the number of exogenous variables can be reduced. From the multipliers in Table 4-1, we know that changes in G_t or S will have no effect on p or y. Also, under fixed exchange rates, $\pi(t-1)$ is constant and thus can be eliminated as an exogenous variable. Hence, equations (4B.1) and (4B.2) can be reduced to

$$p = b_0 + b_2 G_n + b_4 p_t^* + b_5 r^* + b_6 W(t-1) \tag{4B.3}$$

$$y = b_8 + b_{10}G_n + b_{12}p_t^* + b_{13}r^* + b_{14}W(t-1) \qquad (4B.4)$$

The hypothesis is that b_2, $b_{10} > 0$ and we would expect the data to confirm that hypothesis. The multipliers in Table 4-1 do not provide us with any predictions about the signs of the other parameters because p_t^*, r^* and $W(t-1)$ were held constant. Although these parameters are not as crucial as b_2 and b_{10}, some indication of their expected effects on p and y can be given. An increase in the world price of tradables ($dp_t^* > 0$) will lead to an equal increase in the domestic price of tradables and therefore greater output of that commodity. Since this can be accomplished without a reduction in the output of nontradables, real income will rise as well as the overall price level. Therefore, it is to be expected that b_4, $b_{12} > 0$. An increase in the world interest rate ($dr^* > 0$) may be the result of contractionary monetary policy abroad. The effect on the SOE is also contractionary (see the section, ''Changes in the World Interest Rate,'' Chapter 3), and thus we would expect that b_5, $b_{13} < 0$. Finally, an increase in $W(t-1)$ allows for greater expenditures on both tradables and nontradables than would otherwise be the case and hence is expansionary; therefore b_6, $b_{14} > 0$.

Our chief interest in estimating equations (4B.3) and (4B.4) is to derive the effect of changes in fiscal policy in the nontradable sector on prices and income. This is measured by

$$\left(\frac{dp}{dy} \right)_{G_n} = \frac{dp/dG_n}{dy/dG_n} = \frac{b_2}{b_{10}} > 0. \qquad (4B.5)$$

This expression is the slope of the fiscal-policy line in a $p-y$ plane. Since prices are usually measured in index numbers while income is denominated in units of the domestic currency, it may be more appropriate to look at proportional changes rather than absolute changes. This is accomplished by rewriting equation (4B.5) so that the slope of the policy line is $(b_2/b_{10})(y/p)$. If the value of this expression is fairly low, it implies that for a given increase in G_n, there will be a small proportional change in prices, accompanied by a large proportional change in income. Under these circumstances, policy-makers may be content to accept some price increases in order to get closer to full employment. If, on the other hand, the value of this expression is large, they may be reluctant to use fiscal policy as a stabilization instrument. In any case, they will have the necessary information on which to base their decision.

The Reduced-Form Equations Under Flexible Exchange Rates

Unlike the case of fixed exchange rates where empirical estimates of the reduced-form equations will indicate whether or not to use the only available stabilization-policy instrument, under flexible rates, the quantitative estimates of the policy multipliers allow the authorities to use both monetary and fiscal policies to achieve two goals simultaneously: decreased unemployment with a constant price level.

The reduced-form equations for the case of flexible exchange rates are analogous to (4B.1) and (4B.2), namely,

$$p = b_{16} + b_{17}G_t + b_{18}G_n + b_{19}S + b_{20}p_t^*$$
$$+ b_{21}r^* + b_{22}W(t-1) + b_{23}\pi(t-1) \qquad (4B.6)$$

$$y = b_{24} + b_{25}G_t + b_{26}G_n + b_{27}S + b_{28}p_t^*$$
$$+ b_{29}r^* + b_{30}W(t-1) + b_{31}\pi(t-1) \qquad (4B.7)$$

The signs of some of the parameters in equations (4B.6) and (4B.7) are already known from the theoretical results indicated in Table 4-2. For instance, we know that increased government expenditures on tradables have no effect on the price level or real income. Thus $b_{17}, b_{25} = 0$. We also know that $b_{19}, b_{27} > 0$. Furthermore, we could determine the sign of the parameters associated with p_t^*, r^*, $W(t-1)$ and $\pi(t-1)$, in a manner similar to the case of fixed exchange rates. The difficulty arises with the signs of b_{18} and b_{26}, about which we have no *a priori* expectations. We therefore require empirical evidence to remove this ambiguity.

It should be noted that the slope of the fiscal-policy line (G_n) in Case I (Figure 4-2) was negative while in Case II (Figure 4-3) it had a positive slope. The actual slope of the policy line for any particular SOE will have elements of both Case I and Case II. This slope is determined by

$$\left(\frac{dp}{dy}\right)_{G_n} = \frac{dp/dG_n}{dy/dG_n} = \frac{b_{18}}{b_{26}} = ? \qquad (4B.8)$$

If b_{18} and b_{26} have the same sign, then $(dp/dy)_{G_n} > 0$, but if they have opposite signs, then $(dp/dy)_{G_n} < 0$. The first situation comes close to Case II while the second situation is better approximated by Case I. In the event that $b_{18} = 0$, fiscal policy in the nontradable sector has no effect on the price level and full employment and constant prices can be achieved with only this one policy instrument, but if $b_{26} = 0$, then fiscal policy is ineffective for stabilization-policy purposes.

At the same time, we can calculate the slope of the monetary-policy line which is

$$\left(\frac{dp}{dy}\right)_S = \frac{dp/dS}{dy/dS} = \frac{b_{19}}{b_{27}} > 0 \qquad (4B.9)$$

according to the theoretical results reported in the first column of Table 4-2. The question now is how should monetary and fiscal policies be combined

Table 4B-1
Policy Combinations to Achieve Higher Income at a Constant Price Level Under Flexible Exchange Rates

Policy Instrument	Direction of Policy			
	$(dp/dy)_{G_n} < 0$		$(dp/dy)_{G_n} > 0$	
	$b_{26} > 0$	$b_{26} < 0$	$\left(\dfrac{dp}{dy}\right)_{G_n} > \left(\dfrac{dp}{dy}\right)_s$	$\left(\dfrac{dp}{dy}\right)_{G_n} < \left(\dfrac{dp}{dy}\right)_s$
Monetary Policy	(+)	(+)	(+)	(−)
Fiscal Policy	(+)	(−)	(−)	(+)

Note: (+) implies expansionary policy, while (−) implies contractionary policy.

to move the economy closer to full employment while maintaining a constant price level? All possible combinations are considered in Table 4B-1.

To determine the appropriate combination of policies for any particular SOE, the slope of the fiscal-policy line must first be calculated. If it is negative, then b_{26} having both positive and negative values must be considered. In both cases, monetary policy should be expansionary, but if $b_{26} > 0$, then expansionary fiscal policy should be pursued since it puts downward pressure on the price level while allowing income to expand. If, on the other hand, $b_{26} < 0$, contractionary fiscal policy will bring about the same result. If the slope of the fiscal-policy line is positive, it then becomes crucial to compare the slope of this line and that of the monetary policy line. If the former is steeper than the latter, monetary policy should be expansionary but fiscal policy should be contractionary. The opposite policy prescription is called for if $(dp/dy)_{G_n} < (dp/dy)_s$.

Some General Problems of Estimating the Reduced-Form Equations

While it is impossible to set out in detail the precise form of the reduced-form equations to be estimated, some problems which are of a general nature can be discussed.

1. Definition of Government Expenditures on Tradables and Nontradables

One of the main advantages of estimating the reduced-form equations over the procedure of estimating the structure of equations (4.30) to (4.43) is that the distinction between tradables and nontradables need not be made except for the case of government expenditures. In general, it is suggested that wage and salary payments (the largest portion of government expenditures on a national accounts basis in most countries) be considered as expenditures on nontradables. Added to this category should be any expenditures on construction and other goods and services which are clearly nontradables, the residual being expenditures on tradables. In practice, this distinction is not easy to make.

Another difficulty arises from the assumption made in Chapter 4 about the financing of these expenditures, namely that all expenditures were deficit financed. However, even if taxes are levied to finance government activity in whole or in part, it is suggested that the expenditures themselves be used as the appropriate variable rather than that part of the expenditures financed by the issue of government bonds. The reason for this procedure is that as long as tax revenues respond to the level of income, they are endogenous to the system, but the requirement of reduced-form equations is that only exogenous variables appear on the right-hand side. Alternatively, the tax rate, a policy variable, could be included as an independent variable in addition to government expenditures in the two categories.

2. Short-Run vs. Long-Run Multipliers

The model depicted in Chapter 4 and the multipliers derived therefrom deal with the short run, during which time it can reasonably be assumed that wages are "sticky." Even if it can be decided that quarterly or annual data best approximate the short run, estimation of equations (4B.3) and (4B.4) or (4B.6) and (4B.7) will not directly yield the short-run multipliers. This complication arises because exogenous events occurring during time period (t) will continue to have effects on the endogenous variables (p and y) during $(t + 1)$ and beyond and these effects will be captured by the values of p and y in the subsequent periods. Therefore, it is necessary to take into account the possible existence of lags in the adjustment of p or y to any exogenous shocks including changes in the policy variables. The most general solution to this problem is to incorporate Almon lags into the estimating equations.

This procedure involves the *a priori* selection for each variable of the degree of the polynomial which best approximates the expected pattern of the lag structure and the end period of the lag pattern at which point it is assumed that no further response in the dependent variable is anticipated. For the ith variable, $\Sigma_{j=0} b_{ij}$ indicates the total effect on the dependent variable after the jth period. This period of time may be longer than the short run, in which case the sum is truncated at the appropriate point. For instance, using quarterly data, it may be found that events earlier than $(t - 8)$ no longer influence the dependent variable in time period (t). However, two years may be considered to be beyond the short run which is assumed to be only about one year. Thus the accumulated effect for the first four quarters is measured by $\sum_{j=0}^{3} b_{ij}$. In this case, the slope of the fiscal policy line under flexible exchange rates is measured by

$$\left(\frac{dp}{dy} \right)_{G_n} = \frac{\sum\limits_{j=0}^{3} b_{18, j}}{\sum\limits_{j=0}^{3} b_{22, j}}. \tag{4B.10}$$

3. Adjustment for Changes in the Level of Unemployment

A critical assumption in the analysis of policy effectiveness in this study is that the economy has sufficient unemployed resources for the production of nontradables to increase after some exogenous increase in demand without a reduction in the output of tradables and vice versa. Therefore, one would want to estimate the reduced-form equations for a period of time where this proposition is a reasonable approximation of the facts. But except for the 1930s, it is difficult to think of a long enough period during which the level of unemployment was high and constant. As an economy approaches full employment, the multipliers are quantitatively different from those at some high level of unemployment. For instance, under both exchange rate regimes, an increase in government expenditures on nontradables at full employment cannot increase real income. Thus $dy/dG_n = 0$. To take into account the changes in the level of unemployment during the period to be estimated, it might appear worthwhile to multiply each independent variable by the rate of unemployment (u). Therefore, under flexible exchange rates, for instance, $dy/dG_n = b_{26}u$. If $u = 0$, then $dy/dG_n = 0$. The higher is the rate of unemployment the larger will the multiplier be. However, this approach does not take into account the asymmetry involved in this situation. It is possible for an SOE to be accidentally at full employment, even with a "sticky" wage, if that wage just happens to clear the labor market. Expansionary fiscal policy would not increase real income, but contractionary fiscal policy would in fact decrease real income. Thus, $dy/dG_n = 0$ for $dG_n > 0$, but $dy/dG_n \neq 0$ for $dG_n < 0$. Therefore, this procedure may be of doubtful value and it may be better to indicate that the estimates of the multipliers are biased because they do not take into account the variations in the rate of unemployment and are in addition only applicable to the average rate during the period.

The Relationship Between the Reduced-Form Equations
and the Monetarist-Fiscalist Controversy

The models discussed in Chapter 4 are , as pointed out earlier, neutral in the controversy between monetarists and fiscalists that has raged during the past few years. But a similarity between the reduced-form equations suggested here and those used by the adversaries in the controversy cannot go unnoticed. Of special interest in this comparison are the results reported by M. W. Keran[1] of the monetary and fiscal influences on GNP for the United States, Canada, Japan, and a number of European countries. Many of these countries are not SOEs, but Canada comes close enough to warrant treatment as such. He employs reduced-form equations similar to those described above, except that exogenous variables other than monetary and fiscal impulses are omitted and GNP is in nominal terms. This construction of the model does not permit separating the effects of policy changes on prices and real income. The time period chosen for investigation is generally from 1953 to 1968. This choice is particularly unfortunate for the examination of the Canadian experience, since it combines both a period of flexible exchange rates (until 1962) and a period of fixed exchange rates (after 1962). Even a cursory knowledge of Mundell's theoretical results would dictate that separate equations for each time period should be used. Although he found monetary influences to be significant for the whole time period while fiscal influences were not, it is likely that this result would only be duplicated for the period 1953-62, while the conclusions would be reversed for the period 1962-68.

Note

1. M. W. Keran, "Monetary and Fiscal Influences on Economic Activity: The Foreign Experience," *Federal Reserve Bank of St. Louis Review* 52 (1970):16-28.

5

A Devaluation Model of a
Small Open Economy

Introduction

Policy-determined changes in the exchange rate represent another instrument in the arsenal of the policy-makers of the small open economy, in addition to monetary and fiscal policies. They may, therefore, be employed for domestic stabilization purposes, either alone or in conjunction with one or both of the other policies. In a sense, the analysis of this chapter is a continuation of the discussion of policy effectiveness in the previous chapter, where unemployment in part of the labor force prevailed in the absence of policy action, at least temporarily, because of "sticky" wages. But a devaluation or revaluation of the domestic currency may take place even if full employment is guaranteed by a flexible wage. For instance, the domestic authorities may want to insulate the SOE from a one-time increase in the world price of tradables. As we shall see, they accomplish this goal by revaluing the domestic currency to the same extent as the increase in the world prices.

Until recently, the major focus of devaluation models has been on the effect of a change in the exchange rate on the trade balance. However, the introduction of portfolio analysis into balance-of-payments theory has rendered nugatory the emphasis on stability conditions in the foreign exchange market. Once portfolio or wealth adjustments are taken into account, a devaluation cannot lead to a continuing surplus in the balance of payments or the trade balance. Static equilibrium in these models requires that all asset demands are satisfied which implies that capital flows are reduced to zero and that wealth is constant over time, which in turn requires the trade balance to be zero (assuming that other potential sources of growth of domestic private wealth such as government deficits or positive net investment do not exist). In a growing economy, these constraints no longer apply since the acquisition of new assets may be from domestic or foreign sources. In this case, capital flows are consistent with equilibrium, as is a nonzero trade balance. But even in a growing economy, it is not clear that the traditional role of the exchange rate is resurrected. Assume that wealth in the home country is growing at a faster rate than abroad. This leads to capital outflows as well as to a trade deficit. A devaluation may temporarily reduce this deficit, but in the long run the growth of the economy will reassert itself and the balance of payments will move along its original path.[1]

Nevertheless, even in a stationary-state model the exchange rate still has an important role to play, particularly in small open economies. As will be shown in this chapter, the exchange rate influences the price level and aggregate output, if an underemployment equilibrium exists. In that case, devaluation can become a tool of stabilization policy, especially if monetary and fiscal policies are unavailable for this purpose. But, policy-determined changes in the exchange rate may take place when full employment prevails as well as at less-than-full employment. In Chapter 2, the effect of changes in the exchange rate on the factor and commodity markets of a fully-employed SOE were investigated. Similarly, in Chapter 3, the role of the exchange rate in the asset markets was explored. All that needs to be done in the present context is to integrate the discussion into a general equilibrium framework. Then, the impact effects in a stabilization-policy model, where unemployed resources exist, will be investigated. Finally, combinations of monetary, fiscal, and exchange rate policies will be analyzed.

Perfect Capital Mobility and Devaluation

The assumption of perfect capital mobility, first introduced in Chapter 3, has been an integral part of the structure of an SOE. It requires some further clarification in the context of a devaluation model. In a situation of fixed exchange rates, assumed to prevail indefinitely, domestic and foreign bonds can be considered to be perfect substitutes (in the absence of other differences in risk) and their yields will be equalized. Policy-determined changes in the exchange rate, on the other hand, will render the perfect substitutability of the two types of bonds in doubt. In particular, a devaluation of the domestic currency results in a capital loss to foreigners holding domestic bonds. Thus, if the devaluation is anticipated, foreign holders will attempt to rid themselves of domestic bonds in order to prevent such a capital loss. In addition, domestic wealth holders will experience capital gains on any holdings of foreign bonds. For both these reasons the price of domestic bonds will fall relative to the price of foreign bonds, resulting in an interest differential between them. In addition, the changes in wealth caused by the devaluation will alter expenditures temporarily to the extent that there now exists a difference between desired and actual wealth.

In order to maintain the assumption of perfect capital mobility, the following assertions will be made:

a. Domestic residents do not hold foreign bonds. Thus a devaluation will not change the nominal value of domestic wealth.

b. Foreigners *do* hold any excess supply of domestic bonds but the change in foreign wealth will not alter future holdings of domestic bonds nor foreign expenditures. Since the rest of the world is large, foreign holdings of domestic bonds will be a small proportion of total foreign wealth and any change in the value of this component can be considered inconsequential.

c. Devaluations are not anticipated; hence there will be no speculative capital flows.

The first two assumptions have been explicit in the analysis of the previous chapters, but assumption c. requires further comment. It was pointed out in Chapter 3 that perfect capital mobility was possible under either fixed or flexible exchange rates. In both cases, it implied that the domestic interest rate is identical to the world interest rate in full equilibrium. Only during the initial impact period was it possible for the domestic interest rate to differ from the world interest rate when flexible exchange rates prevail because the forward and spot rates will diverge. Therefore, assumption c. is not strictly necessary if we are interested only in the full equilibrium effects of a devaluation. Whether a change in the exchange rate is anticipated or not, after all adjustments have ceased, desired and actual wealth in the SOE will be equal; expenditures will equal income; and the exchange rate being constant at a new level will not call forth expectations of a future rate (equal to the forward rate) different from the spot rate, resulting in an equalization of the unhedged domestic and world interest rates. Only in terms of the initial impact of a devaluation might speculators' expectations result in a future rate different from the spot rate, if the devaluation is anticipated, leading to a temporary difference between the domestic and world interest rates. Normally, devaluations or revaluations are anticipated if a country has a sizeable and persistent deficit or surplus in its balance of payments. But in a static equilibrium model of a small open economy, deficits or surpluses are temporary and self-correcting, requiring no change in the exchange rate to reestablish equilibrium. It may be that speculators will still be able to anticipate changes in the exchange rate if they know for what purposes policy-makers will consider devaluation or revaluation as a legitimate policy tool, but so as not to increase the taxonomy of the analysis, this possibility will be left unexplored.

Devaluation in a Full-Employment Context

Without replicating the algebraic analysis of Chapters 2 and 3, it is possible to outline the effects of a devaluation on the commodity, factor, and asset markets. Assume that the SOE is in full equilibrium at the moment in time before the devaluation. This means that desired and actual wealth positions coincide, implying that domestic residents do not save, but instead spend their entire income on tradables and nontradables. As well, they are satisfied with the composition of their wealth, holding optimal amounts of money and bonds. Throughout the analysis, it is assumed that rates of return to factors of production adjust so as to guarantee their full employment. For simplicity, it is also assumed that the government maintains a balanced budget (implying no expenditures on tradables and nontradables) and that open-market operations by the central bank are absent (implying that the supply of money can only adjust through changes in international reserves).

A devaluation will raise the domestic price of exportables and importables by the same proportion. This result serves to guarantee that both factor rewards as well as the price of nontradables will also rise to the same extent.[a] Therefore, there have been no changes in relative prices, either in the factor markets or the commodity markets. This implies that the economy will remain in its original position on the transformation curve, continuing to produce the same quantities of tradables and nontradables as before. Only an increase in the absolute price level has been generated by the devaluation. But this fact creates disequilibrium in the asset markets because real wealth will now be at a level below that desired by the residents of the SOE. This divergence between desired and actual wealth generates forces that have their impact on both the commodity and asset markets. In an attempt to recoup their wealth position, domestic residents must save a portion of their income, causing expenditures to fall below income. What is not purchased by domestic residents is now bought by foreigners, leading to a positive trade balance. By the same token, the saving allows the SOE to accumulate assets. With the world interest rate remaining constant, both more money and bonds will be demanded, but the demand for money rises by a larger proportion than the demand for bonds since a higher price level requires larger transactions balances. The residents of the SOE obtain the bonds directly from foreigners, resulting in a capital-account deficit while the money is obtained indirectly by running a balance-of-payments surplus, which requires the central bank to absorb the excess foreign currency in exchange for domestic money.

The excess of income over expenditures continues only as long as desired wealth is suboptimal. As soon as desired and actual wealth are again equal, saving disappears and all income is expended. The trade balance is reduced to zero and capital flows cease, leading to overall balance-of-payments equilibrium. In short, asset holders are again satisfied with their portfolios.

In the new final equilibrium, the price level has increased by the extent of the devaluation. As a result, *nominal* wealth, income, expenditures, and

---

[a]See the discussion in the section, "The Exchange Rate and Relative Prices," Chapter 2.

factor returns will also be higher in the same proportion, but the real magnitudes in the economy remain unchanged.[2]

Aside from the temporary effects of a devaluation on these real magnitudes—effects which may be considered desirable or undesirable, under what circumstances is exchange-rate policy useful? Without going into great detail, a number of situations can be mentioned.

1. Since the domestic price level is determined both by the exchange rate and by world prices, price stability can be maintained in the SOE in the face of a rise in world prices by revaluing the domestic currency.

2. To the extent that the central bank has an international reserves target, any deviations from it can be corrected by a change in the exchange rate. As shown above, there is a link between international reserves and the exchange rate through the latter's effect on the demand for money and the former's determination of the money supply.

3. If the domestic authorities are worried about the level of the SOEs' international indebtedness as measured by the stock of domestic bonds held by foreigners, a devaluation may be in order since this increases the domestic demand for bonds and in the absence of government deficits in the SOE, repurchasing bonds from foreigners is the only way this increased demand can be satisfied.

Devaluation as a Stabilization-Policy Instrument

We now turn to the case of an SOE where unemployed labor exists in equilibrium, at least temporarily, and investigate the impact effects of exchange rate policy on output and the price level in much the same way as was done in Chapter 4 for monetary and fiscal policies.

For convenience, the notation describing the variables is repeated here.

p_t, p_n = domestic price of tradables and nontradables, set initially equal to one by an appropriate choice of quantity units

p_t^* = world price of tradables in a numeraire currency

π = exchange rate (that is, price of foreign currency in terms of the domestic currency), set initially equal to one

p = aggregate price level

A_t, A_n = domestic private demand for tradables and nontradables, in quantity terms

Q_t, Q_n = domestic output of tradables and nontradables, in quantity terms

G_t, G_n = government expenditures on tradables and nontradables, in value terms

E, Y = nominal level of domestic private expenditures and income

y = real level of income or output

B = trade balance, in value terms

S, R = central bank holdings of government securities and international reserves ($S + R$ equals the money supply)

$V - V^*$ = value of government bonds held by domestic residents

r^* = world rate of interest (equal to the domestic interest rate)

W, $\overline{W}$ = actual and desired levels of nominal wealth of domestic residents.

The equations of the model are as follows:

$$p_t A_t(p_t, p_n, E) + G_t + B = p_t Q_t(p_t) \tag{5.1}$$

$$Y = p_t Q_t + p_n Q_n \tag{5.2}$$

$$Y - E = G_t + G_n + B \tag{5.3}$$

$$S + R = f(Y/W, r^*)W \tag{5.4}$$

$$W = S + R + V - V^* \tag{5.5}$$

$$E = Y - \gamma[\overline{W} - W(t - 1)] \tag{5.6}$$

$$\overline{W} = \mu Y \tag{5.7}$$

$$y = Y/p \tag{5.8}$$

$$p = \theta_t p_t + (1 - \theta_t)p_n \tag{5.9}$$

$$p_t = \pi p_t^* \tag{5.10}$$

Since these equations were described in detail in the section, "The Complete Stabilization-Policy Model of an SOE," Chapter 4, they require no further elucidation here, except to point out that, unlike the case of fixed exchange rates where π is constant or unlike the case of flexible exchange rates where π is endogenously determined, in this context, π is a policy variable. Also, on the basis of the discussion in this chapter's section, "Perfect Capital Mobility and Devaluation," the world and domestic interest rates are always equal, allowing the former to be substituted for the latter in equation (5.4). Finally, the equilibrium conditions for the nontradable sector and the bond market are again redundant, because they are not independent of other conditions specified in the model.

In terms of differentials (holding r^* and p_t^* constant), these equations can be written as:

$$(A_t + A'_{t,\,p_t} - Q_t - Q'_t)dp_t + A'_{t,\,p_n}\,dp_n$$
$$+ A'_{t,\,E}dE + dG_t + dB = 0 \tag{5.1'}$$

$$dY = (Q_t + Q'_t)dp_t + (Q_n + Q'_n)dp_n \tag{5.2'}$$

$$dY - dE = dG_t + dG_n + dB \tag{5.3'}$$

$$dS + dR = f'_{Y/W}dY + (f - f'_{Y/W}Y/W)dW \tag{5.4'}$$

$$dW = dG_t + dG_n + dB \tag{5.5'}$$

$$dE = dY - \gamma d\overline{W} \tag{5.6'}$$

$$d\overline{W} = \mu dY \tag{5.7'}$$

$$dy = dY - Ydp \tag{5.8'}$$

$$dp = \theta_t dp_t + (1 - \theta_t)dp_n \tag{5.9'}$$

$$dp_t = d\pi \tag{5.10'}$$

It should be noted that the transition from (5.5) to (5.5′) involves the same derivation as required for equation (4.48). This system of 10 equations contains an equal number of endogenous variables: dp_t, dp_n, dE, dB, dY, dR, dW, $d\overline{W}$, dy, and dp. The exogenous variables are all policy determined: dG_t and dG_n for fiscal policy, dS for monetary policy, and $d\pi$ for exchange rate policy.

By a process of substitution, this system is reduced to

$$\begin{bmatrix} \beta_2 & A'_{t,\,E}(1-\gamma\mu) & 1 & 0 \\ f'_{Y/W}Y(1-\theta_t) & f'_{Y/W} & (f - f'_{Y/W}Y/W) & -1 \\ -Q'_n & 1 & 0 & 0 \\ \gamma\mu Y(1-\theta_t) & \gamma\mu & -1 & 0 \end{bmatrix} \begin{bmatrix} dp_n \\ dy \\ dB \\ dR \end{bmatrix}$$

$$= \begin{bmatrix} -dG_t - \beta_1\,d\pi \\ dS - (f - f'_{Y/W}Y/W)\,(dG_t + dG_n) - f'_{Y/W}Y\theta_t d\pi \\ Q'_t\,d\pi \\ dG_t + dG_n - \gamma\mu Y\theta_t\,d\pi \end{bmatrix} \tag{5.11}$$

where
$$\beta_1 = A_t + A'_{t,\,p_t} - Q_t - Q'_t + A'_{t,\,E}(1 - \gamma\mu)Y\theta_t$$
$$= A_t(1 + \eta_{A_t,\,p_t}) - Q_t[1 - A'_{t,\,E}(1 - \gamma\mu)] - Q'_t < 0$$

as long as

$$\eta_{A_t, p_t} < -1$$

and

$$\beta_2 = A'_{t, p_n} + A'_{t, E}(1 - \gamma\mu)Y(1 - \theta_t) > 0$$

Denoting Δ as the determinant of (5.11),

$$\Delta = \gamma\mu Q'_n + \gamma\mu Y(1 - \theta_t) + \beta_2 + Q'_n A'_{t, E}(1 - \gamma\mu) > 0$$

In calculating the initial or impact effects of a devaluation on the endogenous variables over the arbitrary period $(t - 1)$ to (t), it is assumed that the economy starts at full equilibrium (except the labor market, where unemployment exists). I continue to assume that devaluations are not anticipated and that foreigners absorb any capital losses (presumably small in relation to their total wealth), without making any further adjustments. Also, in the subsequent discussion, unless explicitly stated otherwise, it is assumed that $dG_t = dG_n = dS = 0$.

The effect of a devaluation on the price of nontradables can be calculated as follows:

$$\frac{dp_n}{d\pi} = \frac{1}{\Delta} \left[(Q_t + Q'_t) (1 - \gamma\mu) (1 - A'_{t, E}) \right.$$

$$\left. - A_t (1 + \eta_{A_t, p_t}) \right] \tag{5.12}$$

If $\eta_{A_t, p_t} < -1$, then $dp_n/d\pi > 0$. But the price of nontradables can rise more or less than the price of tradables or the exchange rate. This is in contrast to the full-employment case where devaluation did not result in a change in relative prices (that is, $dp_n/d\pi = 1$).

The effect of a devaluation on the price of nontradables has an important impact on R. I. McKinnon's optimum currency argument.[3] In his analysis, domestic price stability is an important objective. He suggests that a devaluation which increases the price of tradables will also increase the overall price index depending on the size of the tradable sector. However, by assumption, "The price of the non-tradable good . . . is kept constant in terms of the domestic currency."[4] This is accomplished by changing domestic expenditures through the application of other policies. For $dp_n = 0$, it can be shown that the required change in government expenditures on nontradables (the only effective instrument for this purpose) is

$$dG_n = [A_t(1 + \eta_{A_t, p_t}) - (Q_t + Q'_t) (1 - \gamma\mu) (1 - A'_{t, E})]d\pi \tag{5.13}$$

Since the expression in the square brackets is negative, G_n should be decreased in order to clear the nontradable market at the original price. In any case, changes in the price level (p) are no longer the result of changes in the exchange rate only, but depend on both expenditure-switching and expenditure-reducing policies. In McKinnon's model

$$\frac{dp}{d\pi} = \theta_t \tag{5.14}$$

as derived from equation (5.9), assuming $dp_n = 0$. The larger is θ_t, the greater is the effect on the price level of a given devaluation. He concludes that a currency area with a large tradable sector is not an optimum currency area since it would sacrifice the objective of price stability. However, by assuming that $dp_n/d\pi = 0$, a second dimension of the problem has been neglected. The effect of a devaluation on the price level is dependent on both the size of the tradable sector and the change in the price of nontradables brought about by the devaluation. In terms of equation (5.9'), the effect of a devaluation on the price level is measured by

$$\frac{dp}{d\pi} = \theta_t + (1 - \theta_t) \frac{dp_n}{d\pi} \tag{5.15}$$

Let Ω be the measure of price stability $(\Omega = dp/d\pi)$. Then differentiating (5.15) with respect to θ_t

$$\frac{\partial \Omega}{\partial \theta_t} = 1 - \frac{dp_n}{d\pi} + (1 - \theta_t) \frac{\partial (dp_n/d\pi)}{\partial \theta_t} \tag{5.16}$$

where $\partial(dp_n/d\pi)/\partial\theta_t$ can be shown to be negative. It is no longer clear that a decrease in the size of the tradable sector will result in greater price stability. This will occur only if $\partial\Omega/\partial\theta_t > 0$. In general, McKinnon underestimates the impact of a devaluation on price stability by arbitrarily holding constant the price of nontradables.

We can now analyze devaluation as a stabilization-policy instrument by determining its effect on real income or output.

$$\frac{dy}{d\pi} = \frac{1}{\Delta} [\gamma\mu Q_n Q_t' + \beta_2 Q_t' + Q_n'\{Q_t (1 - \gamma\mu) (1 - A_{t,E}')$$

$$+ Q_t' - A_t(1 + \eta_{A_t,p_t})\}] > 0 \tag{5.17}$$

It is not surprising that an economy with unemployed resources will experience an increase in total output as indicated by equation (5.17). Since the price of both tradables and nontradables has risen, the supply of each will also increase.[b]

[b]This assumes that $dp_n/d\pi > 0$.

Normally, devaluation is eschewed as a policy instrument to increase aggregate demand since it is a "begger-my-neighbor" policy and invites retaliation. This arises from the fact that in the standard devaluation analysis the increase in aggregate demand involves an improvement in the trade balance offset by an equal decline in the trade balance of other countries and hence results in a reduction in foreign aggregate demand. But devaluation by an SOE does not have this stigma attached since by its very nature an SOE cannot adversely affect aggregate demand in the rest of the world. In this light, devaluation is a legitimate policy instrument, particularly if monetary and fiscal policies are partially or completely inoperative. Nevertheless, it is unlikely that an economy can be "fine-tuned" through this mechanism, for if the exchange rate is adjusted frequently and in response to deviations of the level of aggregate demand from some target level, speculators will come to anticipate these changes giving rise to speculative capital flows which may exacerbate the problem of economic stabilization.

With a higher price level and increased real income, domestic residents will want to hold a larger amount of nominal wealth. This requires that private expenditures be reduced to a level below income which generates the necessary saving to close the gap between desired and actual wealth. In the absence of changes in monetary or fiscal policies, wealth accumulation involves a trade surplus. Thus, in the initial adjustment period,

$$\frac{dB}{d\pi} = \frac{\gamma\mu}{\Delta} \; [\beta_2(Q_t + Q_t') - \beta_1 Q_n'$$

$$+ \; Q_n\{(Q_t + Q_t') \, (1 - A_{t,E}' \, (1 - \gamma\mu))$$

$$- \; A_t(1 + \eta_{A_t, p_t})\} + A_{t,E}'(1 - \gamma\mu)Q_t Q_n']$$
$$> 0 \tag{5.18}$$

if $\eta_{A_t, p_t} < -1$. Ultimately, the trade balance will again be reduced to zero if deficit spending by the government is absent.

If devaluation is used as a stabilization instrument, than it essentially substitutes for open-market operations.[5] Although a devaluation cannot bring about a continuous improvement in the balance of payments, it can cause a once-and-for-all change in the level of reserves and thus an equal change in the domestic money supply. The change in the level of reserves can best be expressed in terms of previously calculated multipliers.

$$\frac{dR}{d\pi} = f_{Y/W}' \frac{dy}{d\pi} + f_{Y/W}' Y\theta_t + f_{Y/W}' \, Y(1 - \theta_t) \, \frac{dp_n}{d\pi}$$

$$+ \; (f - f_{Y/W}' Y/W) \; \frac{dB}{d\pi} > 0 \tag{5.19}$$

The level of reserves will rise because, with an increase in income and prices, the demand for money balances will also rise. In the absence of domestic open-market operations ($dS = 0$), the excess demand for money can only be satisfied through a balance-of-payments surplus. This surplus is generated by the fact that the excess demand for money puts upward pressure on the interest rate forcing it to deviate from the world level. Because of perfect capital mobility, the domestic interest rate will return to its original level through foreign purchases of domestic bonds. This capital inflow creates excess supply of foreign exchange that is absorbed by the central bank in exchange for domestic money. The surplus in the balance of payments disappears when the demand for money is satisfied.

Combining Devaluation with Monetary and Fiscal Policies

So far it has been shown that a devaluation will expand income in an SOE with idle resources. This suggests that a policy-determined adjustment in the exchange rate represents a stabilization-policy instrument. But a devaluation by itself increases both output and prices, forcing the authorities to sacrifice either price stability or full employment. This is the same problem faced by policy-makers who are committed to a fixed exchange rate, but have at their disposal monetary and fiscal policies as stabilization instruments. This situation was discussed in the section, "Stabilization-Policy Effectiveness Under Fixed Exchange Rates," Chapter 4.[c] On the other hand, a regime of flexible exchange rates allowed the authorities to combine monetary and fiscal policies so as to increase output but with stable prices. The question now is whether devaluation together with fiscal or monetary policies can achieve the same result.

To answer this question, we must first calculate the effects of changes in monetary or fiscal policies on y and p. Using (5.11) for this purpose, we find that the only nonzero multipliers are

$$\frac{dy}{dG_n} = \frac{1}{\Delta} \, Q'_n > 0 \tag{5.20}$$

$$\frac{dp_n}{dG_n} = \frac{1}{\Delta} > 0 \tag{5.21}$$

Therefore from (5.9')

$$\frac{dp}{dG_n} = (1 - \theta_t) \, \frac{1}{\Delta} \tag{5.22}$$

---

[c]It will be remembered that monetary policy had no effect on either income or the price level, leaving only fiscal policy to cope with two inconsistent goals.

Dividing (5.20) into (5.22), we obtain

$$\left(\frac{dp}{dy} \right)_{Gn} = \frac{(1 - \theta_t)}{Q'_n} > 0 \qquad (5.23)$$

Thus, expansionary fiscal policy in the nontradable sector increases output and the price level much the same as a devaluation. But, these two policies may have differential effects on income and prices. Therefore, dividing (5.17) into (5.15) shows that $(dp/dy)_\pi > 0$. In general, it is not possible to determine whether $(dp/dy)_{G_n}$ is larger or smaller than $(dp/dy)_\pi$. (It would be purely coincidental for them to be equal.) Both situations are depicted in Figure 5-1.

The aim of the policy-maker is to move the economy from X to X', that is to expand output at a constant price level using fiscal policy in the nontradable sector and exchange rate policy. The arrow on the π line indicates the movement in the p-y plane as a result of a devaluation while the arrow on the G_n line implies expansionary policy. In part (a) of Figure 5-1, where the π line is steeper than the G_n line, the appropriate policy combination is expansionary fiscal policy and a revaluation. In part (b), a devaluation together with contractionary fiscal policy is recommended. Because these policy combinations are diametrically opposed to each other, it is crucial that policy-makers have sufficient information about the structure of the economy for them to decide whether (a) or (b) is the relevant situation. This is much the same problem faced by policy-makers using monetary and fiscal policies under a regime of flexible exchange rates, but again the benefits from improved policy effectiveness are probably worth the cost of obtaining this information.[d]

Notes

1. For an exposition of the balance-of-payments effects of wealth accumulation, see J. A. Frenkel, "A Theory of Money, Trade and the Balance of Payments in a Model of Accumulation," *Journal of International Economics* 1 (1971): 159-87.

---

[d]To derive this information, estimates of reduced-form equations similar to those described in Appendix 4B could be obtained. However, for this purpose we require data for SOEs where devaluations or revaluations have actually occurred in the past. As an alternative, the parameter associated with p_t^* (the foreign price of tradables) could be used as an indication of the effect of a change in the exchange rate, since the domestic price of tradables will increase (decrease), either because the foreign price of tradables has risen (fallen) or because the exchange rate has been increased (decreased).

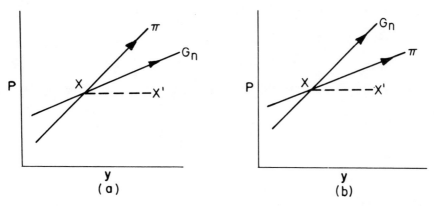

Figure 5-1. Fiscal- and Exchange-Rate Policy Effects on Prices and Income

2. These results may be compared with those derived by Dornbusch, who also formulates a "monetary" model of devaluation. See Rudiger Dornbusch, "Devaluation, Money, and Nontraded Goods," *American Economic Review* 63 (1973): 871-80.

3. R. I. McKinnon, "Optimum Currency Areas," *American Economic Review* 53 (1963): 717-25.

4. Ibid., p. 719.

5. This point is also made by Johnson. See H. G. Johnson, "The Monetary Approach to Balance-of-Payments Theory," in M. B. Connolly and A. K. Swoboda, eds., *International Trade and Money*, London, George Allen and Unwin, 1973, p. 222.

6

The Inflationary Process

Introduction

Throughout most of the previous analysis, the environment external to the small open economy has been one of constancy. In designing optimal policies or policy combinations for domestic economic stabilization, the authorities in the SOE have been able to assume that conditions outside their jurisdiction were stable and unchanging. But this is an unrealistic setting for policy decisions in the world of today. Perhaps most importantly, policy-makers in an SOE must cope with the problem of imported inflation, which involves an exogenously determined rate of growth of prices being transmitted from the rest of the world to the SOE. The SOE cannot influence this rate of inflation but is affected by it. This inflationary process can be transmitted to the SOE by developments in international capital and money markets or through the interaction of goods markets in the SOE with those of the rest of the world or, most likely, through both channels.[1]

Whatever the ultimate cause of world inflation, the only relevant factor for the SOE is that the prices of its tradable goods are rising at a rate over which it has no control. Given this condition, we can then determine the overall rate of inflation in the SOE by analyzing the transmission mechanism, as well as describing the adjustments in the commodity and asset markets necessary to maintain equilibrium. It will also be demonstrated that a flexible exchange rate system is superior to a fixed rate regime in terms of allowing policy-makers of the SOE to have some control over the rate of inflation.

Of significant importance in the analysis of this chapter is the fact that inflation can be generated in an SOE without the conditions normally associated with either market-power inflation or *domestic* demand-pull inflation. All that is necessary is *foreign* excess demand putting upward pressure on the world price of tradables. It is this feature that distinguishes the inflationary process in an SOE from that in a large or closed economy. In order to focus on the special characteristics of a small open economy in an inflationary context, I propose to abstract from the purely domestic inflationary forces associated with the Phillips-curve analysis. Therefore, it will be assumed that all markets (including the labor market) in an SOE are perfectly competitive and adjust instantaneously to external disturbances.

The Transmission Mechanism

In Chapter 2, it was shown that a small open economy is a price-taker with respect to exportable and importable commodities and, in the absence of tariffs or subsidies, the world price of these goods dictated their domestic price, adjusted only for the exchange rate. To investigate the transmission mechanism of externally generated inflation, we can focus on the price equations of that chapter which were initially adapted from Jones.[2] Thus

$$a_{Lx}w + a_{Tx}r = p_x = \pi p_x^* \tag{6.1}$$

$$a_{Lm}w + a_{Tm}r = p_m = \pi p_m^* \tag{6.2}$$

$$a_{Ln}w + a_{Tn}r = p_n \tag{6.3}$$

where p_x, p_m, p_n are the domestic prices of exportables (Q_x), importables (Q_m), and nontradables (Q_n); w and r are the returns to the two factors, labor (L) and land (T); p_x^* and p_m^* are the world prices of Q_x and Q_m, respectively; π is the exchange rate; and the a_{ij}'s are the input requirements of factor i in industry j. These equations assume constant returns to scale and perfect competition in the product markets so that profits are reduced to zero in equilibrium. Taking time derivatives of these equations and denoting ($\tilde{\ }$) as the operator for the proportional rate of change over time [e.g., $\tilde{w} = (\partial w/\partial t)(1/w)$], we obtain relationships similar to those derived by Jones:[3]

$$\theta_{Lx}\tilde{w} + \theta_{Tx}\tilde{r} = \tilde{\pi} + \tilde{p}_x^* + [\theta_{Lx}\tilde{b}_{Lx} + \theta_{Tx}\tilde{b}_{Tx}] \tag{6.4}$$

$$\theta_{Lm}\tilde{w} + \theta_{Tm}\tilde{r} = \tilde{\pi} + \tilde{p}_m^* + [\theta_{Lm}\tilde{b}_{Lm} + \theta_{Tm}\tilde{b}_{Tm}] \tag{6.5}$$

$$\theta_{Ln}\tilde{w} + \theta_{Tn}\tilde{r} = \tilde{p}_n + [\theta_{Ln}\tilde{b}_{Ln} + \theta_{Tn}\tilde{b}_{Tn}] \tag{6.6}$$

where θ_{ij} is the share of the ith factor in the revenue of the jth industry [e.g., $\theta_{Lx} = (w/p_x) a_{Lx}$]. The $\tilde{b}_{ij}$'s may be interpreted as exogenous technical change.[a] If, over time, a smaller amount of factor i is required to produce a unit of j, then $\tilde{b}_{ij} > 0$. Treating $\tilde{p}_x^*$, $\tilde{p}_m^*$, $\tilde{\pi}$ and the $\tilde{b}_{ij}$'s as exogenous, we can solve equations (6.4) and (6.5) for $\tilde{w}$ and $\tilde{r}$ and substituting into equation (6.6), we can derive $\tilde{p}_n$. Without further restrictions, these solutions would be extremely complicated. Therefore, taking a very simple case at first, it is assumed that $\tilde{\pi} = 0$, $\tilde{b}_{ij} = 0$, and $\tilde{p}_x^* = \tilde{p}_m^* = \tilde{p}_t^*$, where p_t^* is the world price of a composite good which aggregates exportables and importables. Under these conditions,

$$\tilde{w} = \tilde{r} = \tilde{p}_n = \tilde{p}_t^* \tag{6.7}$$

---

[a]The $\tilde{b}_{ij}$'s refer to only one component of the time rate of change of the a_{ij}'s. The other component, which deals with the response to changes in relative factor prices, disappears when weighted by the appropriate θ's. See equation (2.22).

In this case, the inflation abroad is completely transmitted to the SOE. Whatever the rate of inflation is in the rest of the world, the same rate will prevail in the domestic economy. There will be no changes in relative factor prices and therefore firms will not substitute one factor for the other; there will also be constant relative commodity prices and therefore consumers will not substitute one commodity for another. However, if the $\tilde{b}_{ij}$'s are not zero and differ among factors or industries, there may be changes in relative factor rewards as well as changes in relative commodity prices.[b]

In order to make the analysis more meaningful, but at the same time less taxonomic, I will concentrate on changes in labor productivity, since it is often argued that for any given rate of *wage* inflation, the higher is the productivity growth of labor, the lower will be the rate of *price* inflation.[4] It is therefore assumed that the world prices of exportables and importables grow at the same rate (that is, $\tilde{p}_x^* = \tilde{p}_m^*$), and that technological change with respect to labor is the same in the two industries (that is, $\tilde{b}_{Lx} = \tilde{b}_{Lm}$). These conditions will later allow us to aggregate exportables and importables into a homogeneous commodity called tradables whose price is p_t. At the same time, productivity of the other factor (T) is assumed to remain constant over time (that is, $\tilde{b}_{Tx} = \tilde{b}_{Tm} = \tilde{b}_{Tn} = 0$). Furthermore, assume that a fixed exchange rate prevails so that it is a matter of indifference whether prices are measured in the domestic or foreign currency (that is, $\tilde{\pi} = 0$ or $\tilde{p}_t^* = \tilde{p}_t$). This restriction will be dropped at a later stage. Finally, it is assumed, as in the earlier analysis, that the production of all three commodities uses only primary factors to avoid difficulties encountered when nontradables are inputs for the two tradable commodities and vice versa.

These assumptions allow us to generate the following results:

$$\tilde{w} = \tilde{p}_t + \tilde{b}_{Lt} \tag{6.8}$$

$$\tilde{r} = \tilde{p}_t \tag{6.9}$$

$$\tilde{p}_n = \tilde{p}_t + \theta_{Ln}(\tilde{b}_{Lt} - \tilde{b}_{Ln}) \tag{6.10}$$

As pointed out earlier, prices in the two tradable industries are given by external conditions. But the growth rate of these two prices in conjunction with productivity improvements will determine uniquely the rate of change of the two factor returns as shown in equations (6.8) and (6.9). Assuming perfect factor mobility between the two tradable industries and the non-tradable sector, the rates of return to both factors are equal everywhere. Unlike in Chapter 4, the money wage is no longer temporarily "sticky." Because of persistent inflation, workers are presumed to offer their ser-

---

[b]These complications would also arise if $\tilde{p}_x^* \neq \tilde{p}_m^*$, in which case exportables and importables could not be aggregated.

vices on the basis of real wages.[c] Now in the nontradable sector, the changes in w and r, together with productivity growth in that sector, determine the growth rate of the price of nontradables as indicated by equation (6.10).

As in Chapter 4, given the assumptions made above, the model is reduced to two sectors: tradables ($Q_t = Q_x + Q_m$) and nontradables (Q_n), with prices p_t and p_n. Starting with equation (4.41) from Chapter 4, which defined the aggregate price level, it is easy to see that the rate of change of the price of total output is a weighted average of the growth rates of the prices of tradables and nontradables. Thus we have the identity

$$\tilde{p} = \theta_t \tilde{p}_t + (1 - \theta_t)\tilde{p}_n \qquad (6.11)$$

where p_t and p_n are the domestic prices of the two goods and $\theta_t = p_t Q_t / Y = (p_t/p)(Q_t/y)$ and $1 - \theta_t = p_n Q_n / Y = (p_n/p)(Q_n/y)$ which represent the fixed value-of-production weights.

As with any index number, treating the weights as constant creates a possible bias in the measurement of $\tilde{p}$ if there are differential rates of inflation in the two sectors. Assume, for instance, that $\tilde{p}_n > \tilde{p}_t$. Thus if θ_t is evaluated in the initial period as with a Laspeyres price index, p_t/p is falling over time and, *ceteris paribus*, θ_t is declining. But at the same time, the other component of θ_t, that is Q_t/y, should be rising as consumers are expanding their demand for tradables at the expense of nontradables in the face of a shift in relative prices. But this incentive to substitute tradables for nontradables may be offset by a higher income elasticity for the latter group of commodities than the former. An interpretation of the evidence provided by H. S. Houthakker on income elasticities for a number of countries seems to lead to that conclusion.[7] Moreover, there may be an upward bias in the price index of services, which make up the bulk of the nontradable sector in most countries, because of the difficulties in measuring quality improvements. But no matter what the difficulties are, there is little choice other than to treat the weights as constant, an assumption which will be retained for the remainder of the discussion.

Substituting (6.10) into (6.11), the overall rate of inflation is determined by the following equation:

$$\tilde{p} = \tilde{p}_t + (1 - \theta_t)\theta_{Ln}(\tilde{b}_{Lt} - \tilde{b}_{Ln}) \qquad (6.12)$$

It should be noted that

$$(1 - \theta_t)\theta_{Ln} = \frac{p_n Q_n}{Y} \frac{L_n}{Q_n} \frac{w}{p_n} = \frac{w L_n}{Y}$$

[c]Money illusion on the part of labor that dissipates over time could be incorporated into the model, but this is a complex issue involving adaptive expectations to the actual rate of inflation and although germane to the topic at hand, its exploration would take us too far afield. For a discussion of some of these ideas, see Milton Friedman[5] and E. S. Phelps.[6]

which represents the ratio of labor income in the nontradable industry to total national income. From equation (6.12), it can be seen that $\bar{p}$ is determined partly by external factors and partly by domestic conditions. Two extreme situations can be defined: inflation is entirely generated from abroad if $\bar{b}_{Lt} = \bar{b}_{Ln}$ and thus $\bar{p} = \bar{p}_t$ or inflation is completely of a domestic nature if $\bar{p}_t = 0$ and $\bar{b}_{Lt} > \bar{b}_{Ln}$.

The external factors enter through $\bar{p}_t$ which is determined exogenously for the SOE. An increase in $\bar{p}_t$ is transmitted entirely to $\bar{p}$ because such an increase raises $\bar{w}$ and $\bar{r}$ in both sectors which in turn leads to an increase in $\bar{p}_n$ by the same proportion. In this context, the size of the tradable sector is not crucial, and *theoretically* a very small tradable sector as measured by θ_t has the same effect as a very large one. However, it should be borne in mind that the transmission mechanism would be hard-pressed if the tradable sector were insignificantly small. Specifically, the competitive adjustment of factor returns may not be possible unless the tradable sector reaches a certain minimum size.

The domestic conditions that influence the overall rate of inflation are θ_t, θ_{Ln}, $\bar{b}_{Lt}$ and $\bar{b}_{Ln}$. Here the size of the tradable sector is important. For any given $\bar{b}_{Lt} - \bar{b}_{Ln} > 0$, the larger is the tradable sector, the smaller will be the effect on $\bar{p}$. It is also interesting to note that the higher is the growth of productivity in the tradable sector, *ceteris paribus*, the higher is the rate of inflation. This appears to be contrary to the notion that increases in productivity tend to hold down the rate of inflation.[d] According to equation (6.12), the way to impede inflation is to encourage productivity increases primarily in the nontradable sector.

In the tradition of the Phillips-curve analysis, only labor-productivity growth has been dealt with explicitly. But, unlike the literature based on Phillips,[8] the wage rate adjustment is not related to the excess demand (or supply) of labor. In a closed economy, wage rates are determined by labor market conditions, including the extent and strength of union bargaining power, mobility of labor, cost of information, etc. Then the rate of growth of the price level is determined by changes in productivity and by the growth rate of wages. But, in an SOE, the process is reversed; price changes are exogenous (at least in the tradable sector) and, in conjunction with productivity growth, they determine wage rate adjustments over time.[e]

---

[d]The contradiction is removed if it is remembered that productivity growth holds down inflation only if wage increases are given. But here price inflation in the tradable sector is given and increased productivity merely increases the rate of wage inflation, which in turn is transmitted to the nontradable sector.

[e]In a recent paper, B. L. Scarfe has attempted to provide the foundation for a Phillips curve in the context of an SOE.[9] He argues that "the potential domestic unemployment rate [related to the actual rate of unemployment with a lag] is an increasing function of the economy's degree of 'non-competitiveness.' This non-competitiveness may be measured by (the natural

In a sense, an SOE faces an externally imposed incomes policy. By taking as exogenous the rate of increase of tradable prices, the overall rate of inflation is determined. It is, of course, possible that this external constraint is higher than that considered optimal, in which case the authorities in the SOE should allow the exchange rate to appreciate over time at a rate which represents the difference between the actual and optimum rates of inflation. This proposition will be developed more fully in the next section.

Inflation and the Exchange Rate

The rate of growth of the price of tradables is only exogenous to the small open economy if it maintains a fixed exchange rate. If, on the other hand, the exchange rate is allowed to float or if the authorities devalue or revalue the domestic currency, then we must distinguish between the price of tradables in the domestic currency and in a numeraire currency. Under these conditions, the price of tradables in the rest of the world, denominated in the numeraire currency is exogenous to the SOE, but the price of tradables in the domestic currency depends on the exchange rate. Hence

$$\tilde{p}_t = \tilde{\pi} + \tilde{p}_t^* \tag{6.13}$$

($\tilde{\pi} > 0$ implies a depreciation of the domestic currency over time.) Substituting (6.13) into (6.12) yields

$$\tilde{p} = \tilde{\pi} + \tilde{p}_t^* + (1 - \theta_t)\,\theta_{Ln}(\tilde{b}_{Lt} - \tilde{b}_{Ln}) \tag{6.14}$$

Now it can be seen that a continuous depreciation of the domestic currency increases the rate of inflation and in fact there is a one-to-one relationship between the two variables.[f]

McKinnon has focused on the problem of imported inflation and suggested that countries should adopt an "optimum gliding parity" to counter these external influences on the domestic price level.[11] According to equation (6.14), in order to obtain $\tilde{p} = 0$, it is necessary that

---

logarithm of) the economy's 'cost ratio''' (p. 193). In terms of our notation, this cost ratio is $(w/\phi_t)/\pi p_t^*$, where ϕ_t is the marginal product of labor in the tradable industry. But, since by assumption, $p_t = w/\phi_t = \pi p_t^*$, this ratio is always equal to one. Although a variable cost ratio may fit in with Scarfe's concept of a small open economy, noncompetitiveness is not compatible with the defintion in this study, where it is explicit that an SOE is a price-taker in the world market for tradables. At home and abroad it charges no more and no less for a unit of tradables than the world price for that commodity. This is the only way it can survive. If a Phillips curve were to be introduced into the analysis, it would appear that it should rely on noncompetitiveness in the labor market rather than in the tradables market.

[f]Egon Sohmen has argued that, in most cases, devaluation does not contribute to inflation.[10] His analysis, however, started from a position of an overvalued currency where external balance was maintained by trade impediments. Then taking into account both a devaluation and removal of the trade barriers, he found that the price level could indeed decline.

$$\tilde{\pi} = -\tilde{p}_t^* - (1 - \theta_t)\theta_{Ln}(\tilde{b}_{Lt} - \tilde{b}_{Ln}) \qquad (6.15)$$

Thus, countries should appreciate their currencies over time in order to offset the inflationary pressures emanating from abroad and at home. For any given level of $\tilde{p}_t^*$, countries with a large differential in the growth of labor productivity between the tradable and nontradable sectors should appreciate their currencies faster than those with a smaller differential, while those with a negative differential might even depreciate their currencies if $-(1 - \theta_t)\theta_{Ln}(\tilde{b}_{Lt} - \tilde{b}_{Ln}) > \tilde{p}_t^*$. This conclusion is somewhat at odds with McKinnon's, who proposes "that countries with fast growth of productivity and only average tolerance for increases in the [Consumer Price Index] should appreciate their currency steadily under a gliding parity."[12] In McKinnon's model, no explicit distinction is made between productivity in the tradable sector and in the nontradable sector. His conclusion is only correct if his statement refers to productivity growth in the former sector.

In summary, the authorities in an SOE with an unalterably fixed exchange rate must treat the overall rate of inflation as given since they cannot influence the growth rate of the world price of tradables and since they are unlikely to be able to control productivity changes in the two sectors, at least in the short run. On the other hand, they have a much better chance of obtaining the desired rate of inflation if they are prepared to allow the exchange rate to adjust in accordance with equation (6.15).

Inflation and the Asset Markets

So far, the inflationary phenomenon has been viewed as a process involving only the price equations of a general equilibrium framework. But whether inflation is an exogenous event, as in the case of fixed exchange rates, or whether the domestic rate of inflation can be forced to be some optimal rate by a system of gliding exchange rates, it will generate a disequilibrium situation in the commodity and asset markets, setting in motion adjustment processes that must be investigated. In this section, the adjustment process in the asset markets will be considered, while the effects of inflation on the commodity markets will be investigated in the next section of this chapter.

In previous chapters, the role of desired real wealth played an important role in the adjustment from one static equilibrium to the next, after an exogenous disturbance to the system. With persistent inflation, this adjustment in desired wealth will be a continuous one. Instead of saving only to close a one-time gap between actual and desired wealth, as was the case in the static analysis of Chapters 4 and 5, in the context of inflation, it is assumed that desired and actual wealth grow at the same rate so that

$$\tilde{W} = \tilde{\bar{W}} \qquad (6.16)$$

where W and $\overline{W}$ are actual and desired levels of nominal wealth. Since saving (that is, the accumulation of wealth) represents the difference between income and expenditure, we have

$$\tilde{W} = \frac{Y - E}{W} \qquad (6.17)$$

As previously, it is assumed that desired real wealth is related to real income so that in terms of growth rates this relationship is expressed as

$$\tilde{\overline{W}} = \tilde{Y} = \tilde{p} + \tilde{y} \qquad (6.18)$$

where $\tilde{y}$ is the growth rate of real income and is exogenous to the asset-market equilibrium.

The composition of wealth depends on the ratio of income to wealth, the level of wealth and the world or domestic interest rate, depending on whether fixed or flexible exchange rates prevail. From Chapter 3, the money-market equilibrium in terms of growth rates can be written as

$$\lambda_{SZ}\tilde{S} + \lambda_{RZ}\tilde{R} = \eta_{f,\,Y/W}(\tilde{p} + \tilde{y}) + (1 - \eta_{f,\,Y/W})\tilde{W} + \eta_{f,r}\tilde{r} \qquad (6.19)$$

where S and R represent central bank holdings of domestic government bonds and international reserves, so that $Z = S + R$ is the total money supply; the λ's refer to the proportion of each component in the total; and the η's refer to elasticities with respect to the subscripted variables. It was assumed in Chapter 3 that $\eta_{f,\,Y/W} < 1$. In the case of fixed exchange rates, $\tilde{r} = 0$ as long as the world interest rate remains constant over time. The *nominal* world interest rate, which is relevant here, is likely to be higher in an inflationary environment than if prices are presumed to remain stable. Thus an increase in $\tilde{p}_t^*$ will increase r^* requiring a once-and-for-all upward adjustment in r.[13] In terms of differentials,

$$dr = dr^* = d\tilde{p}_t^* \qquad (6.20)$$

But this does not change the conclusion that $\tilde{r} = 0$, which stipulates that the domestic interest rate does not change with the passage of time.

If the exchange rate is fixed, equations (6.14) with $\tilde{\pi} = 0$, (6.16), (6.18) and (6.19) with $\tilde{r} = 0$ represent a self-contained system which allows us to explore the effects on the asset markets of an exogenous rate of inflation as well as the role of monetary policy on the inflationary process. (The bond-market equilibrium is omitted from the system because it is determined residually after changes in total wealth and money holdings are known.) By a process of substitution we can solve for $\tilde{R}$:

$$\tilde{R} = \frac{(1 - \theta_t)\theta_{Ln}(\tilde{b}_{Lt} - \tilde{b}_{Ln}) + \tilde{y} + \tilde{p}_t^* - \lambda_{SZ}\tilde{S}}{\lambda_{RZ}} \qquad (6.21)$$

All other factors held constant, an increase in $(\tilde{b}_{Lt} - \tilde{b}_{Ln})$ or $\tilde{y}$ (growth in productivity in the two sectors and growth of real income are really much the same thing, as will be seen later) will increase the growth rate of the central bank's accumulation of international reserves, because these forces lead to a higher growth rate in the demand for money which can only be satisfied through adjustments in the balance of payments. An exogenous increase in $\tilde{p}_t^*$ has the same effect on $\tilde{R}$, but it is worth noting that such an event will lead to a once-and-for-all increase in the domestic interest rate according to equation (6.20), causing domestic residents to make a single shift from money to bonds. The only policy variable in equation (6.21) is $\tilde{S}$, which represents the rate of change of open-market operations over time. While expansionary (contractionary) open-market operations lead to a decumulation (accumulation) of reserves, the total money supply is unaffected by monetary policy. Since $Z = S + R$,

$$\tilde{Z} = \lambda_{SZ}\tilde{S} + \lambda_{RZ}\tilde{R}$$
$$= \lambda_{SZ}\tilde{S} - \lambda_{RZ}(S/R)\tilde{S} = 0 \qquad (6.22)$$

This leads us to the conclusion that domestic monetary policy under fixed exchange rates has no influence on the rate of inflation; the supply of money, being endogenous to the system, adjusts automatically to its demand which responds to the given rate of inflation.

If the exchange rate is allowed to float without intervention by the central bank, the adjustment in the asset markets is somewhat different. Because there is now the possibility of a continuous change in the exchange rate, perfect capital mobility may no longer result in the equalization of the unhedged domestic and world interest rates. If the domestic currency is appreciating over time, foreign holders of domestic bonds will realize a capital gain as well as the interest payments on these bonds. To the extent that these capital gains are anticipated, the domestic interest rate will, in equilibrium, diverge from the world interest rate, so that

$$r - \tilde{\pi} = r^* \qquad (6.23)$$

which specifies that the domestic interest rate plus the capital gains stemming from the appreciation of the domestic currency ($\tilde{\pi} < 0$) equal the world interest rate. The yields on domestic and foreign bonds are now equalized.

From this equation, it is evident that a one-time change in the rate of appreciation or depreciation of the domestic currency will alter the domestic interest rate. (Altering $\tilde{\pi}$ will have no affect on r^*.) To the extent that monetary policy has some influence on $\tilde{\pi}$, it is possible for the SOE to pursue an interest-rate policy independent of events in the rest of the world.

But even more important is the fact that a change in $\tilde{\pi}$ directly influences the rate of inflation.

To find the determinants of $\tilde{\pi}$, we again use equations (6.14), (6.16), (6.18) and (6.19) with $\tilde{R} = \tilde{r} = 0$.[g] A solution of these equations produces

$$\tilde{\pi} = -(1 - \theta_t)\theta_{Ln} (\tilde{b}_{Lt} - \tilde{b}_{Ln}) - \tilde{y} - \tilde{p}_t^* + \lambda_{sz}\tilde{S} \qquad (6.24)$$

In this case, an increase in $(\tilde{b}_{Lt} - \tilde{b}_{Ln})$, $\tilde{y}$ or $\tilde{p}_t^*$, instead of leading to an increase in the accumulation of international reserves, causes a larger appreciation (or a smaller depreciation) of the domestic currency than would otherwise be the case. All of these factors dictate an increase in the growth rate of the demand for money, and since the supply of money does not automatically adjust (assuming $\tilde{S} = 0$), the demand is dampened by a decrease in $\tilde{\pi}$ which reduces the rate of inflation. On the policy side, increasing the growth rate of open-market operations ($\tilde{S}$) will lead to an increase in the rate of depreciation (or a decrease in the rate of appreciation) of the domestic currency. Thus under flexible exchange rates, monetary policy has a direct influence on the rate of inflation in the SOE. A lower rate of inflation is achieved by allowing the supply of money to grow at a rate slower than the rate of growth of demand. This puts continuous upward pressure on the domestic interest rate engendering capital inflows which in turn lead to an excess demand for the domestic currency forcing a continuous decline in the exchange rate.

In Chapter 4, a strong point in favor of flexible exchange rates was the possibility of pursuing a stabilization policy which allowed for an expansion of output and thus a reduction in unemployment together with maintaining a constant price level—a possibility that does not exist in the case of a fixed exchange rate. In the present context of persistent inflation emanating from abroad, we again find that a regime of flexible exchange rates is superior to a fixed exchange rate system, since the former allows the domestic monetary authorities to close any gap between the externally dictated rate of inflation and some optimum rate of growth of the price level by allowing the exchange rate to drift in a manner described above. While an "optimum gliding parity" system as suggested by McKinnon may achieve the same result, it is sufficiently inflexible and administratively complex so that a truly floating exchange rate system may still be preferable.

Inflation and the Commodity Markets

The inflationary process influences the commodity markets directly

---

[g]Although a change in $\tilde{\pi}$ will influence the *level* of r as stipulated by (6.23), $\tilde{r} = 0$ because the interest rate does not increase or decrease continuously over time.

through changes in relative prices caused by the differential growth of labor productivity in the tradable and nontradable sectors and indirectly through the divergence between income and expenditures necessitated by the fact that domestic wealth accumulation takes place to maintain a desired level of real wealth.

The Supply of Tradables and Nontradables

The sources of change over time in the output of tradables and nontradables are: (1) changes in prices, (2) increases in factor availability, and (3) increases in factor productivity. R. W. Jones[14] has pointed out that (2) and (3) have similar effects and therefore I propose to abstract from growth in factor supplies and concentrate on changes in factor productivity. In fact, as before, only growth in labor productivity in the tradable and nontradable sectors will be considered.

The combination of changes in relative commodity prices as well as the growth in labor productivity involve both the Stolper-Samuelson theorem and the Rybczynski theorem. On the one hand, factor productivity (a substitute for factor availability) is growing disproportionately between the two factors, bringing about a magnification effect similar to the Rybczynski theorem. On the other hand, changes in relative prices have a magnified effect on relative factor rewards similar to the Stolper-Samuelson theorem, bringing about factor substitutions in the production process.[h] To analyze this situation, it is again necessary to disaggregate tradables into exportables and importables, but still assuming that $\tilde{p}_x = \tilde{p}_m = \tilde{p}_t$ and $\tilde{b}_{Lx} = \tilde{b}_{Lm} = \tilde{b}_{Lt}$.

For this three-sector model, the growth rates of the outputs are determined by the following equations:

$$\lambda_{Lx}\tilde{Q}_x + \lambda_{Lm}\tilde{Q}_m + \lambda_{Ln}\tilde{Q}_n = \delta_L(\tilde{w} - \tilde{r})$$
$$+ [(\lambda_{Lx} + \lambda_{Lm})\tilde{b}_{Lt} + \lambda_{Ln}\,\tilde{b}_{Ln}] \tag{6.25}$$

$$\lambda_{Tx}\tilde{Q}_x + \lambda_{Tm}\tilde{Q}_m + \lambda_{Tn}\tilde{Q}_n = -\delta_T(\tilde{w} - \tilde{r}) \tag{6.26}$$

These two equations are similar to those used by Jones to investigate the effects of productivity growth.[15] λ_{ij} is the fraction of factor i used in the production of commodity j, while δ_L and δ_T are positive constants previously defined in the section, "The Production Sector," Chapter 2. From equations (6.8) and (6.9) we know that

$$\tilde{w} - \tilde{r} = \tilde{b}_{Lt} \tag{6.27}$$

But even when this result is substituted into (6.25) and (6.26), the system is

---

[h]According to equations (6.8) and (6.9), $\tilde{w} > \tilde{p}_t = \tilde{r}$.

underdetermined. Therefore, it is necessary to specify that the domestic output of nontradables is always equal to its domestic demand. In terms of growth rates,

$$\tilde{Q}_n = \tilde{A}_n = (\eta_{A_n, p_x} + \eta_{A_n, p_m})\tilde{p}_t + \eta_{A_n, p_n}\tilde{p}_n + \eta_{A_n, E}\tilde{E} \qquad (6.28)$$

which is similar to equation (2.31). This equation introduces two more variables, $\tilde{p}_n$ and $\tilde{E}$. To close the system, equation (6.10) is used as well as the assumption that income and expenditures grow at the same rate, a proposition to be proven in the next section. Thus

$$\tilde{E} = \tilde{Y} = \tilde{y} + \tilde{p} \qquad (6.29)$$

But according to an equation derived by Jones,[16]

$$\tilde{y} = \theta_x\tilde{Q}_x + \theta_m\tilde{Q}_m + \theta_n\tilde{Q}_n = \theta_L\tilde{L} + \theta_T\tilde{T} \qquad (6.30)$$

where the θ's are distributive shares of each commodity or factor in income. Although, by assumption, factor supplies are fixed, productivity improvements in labor substitute directly for $\tilde{L}$ while $\tilde{T} = 0$. Thus

$$\tilde{y} = \theta_L[(\lambda_{Lx} + \lambda_{Lm})\tilde{b}_{Lt} + \lambda_{Ln}\tilde{b}_{Ln}] \qquad (6.31)$$

By a process of substitution into equation (6.28), the following result is derived:[i]

$$\tilde{Q}_n = \tilde{A}_n = (\theta_{Ln}\eta_{A_n, p_n} + \theta_L\eta_{A_n, E})\tilde{b}_{Lt} - \theta_{Ln}\eta_{A_n, p_n}\tilde{b}_{Ln} \qquad (6.32)$$

According to this equation, an increase in $\tilde{b}_{Ln}$ unambiguously increases the rate of growth of demand for, and output of, nontradables since $\eta_{A_n, p_n} < 0$. But an increase in $\tilde{b}_{Lt}$ has ambiguous effects since the sign of the expression in the first parentheses is indeterminate. This result can be explained by the fact that an increase in $\tilde{b}_{Lt}$ also increases income allowing consumers to buy more of all three commodities but at the same time it causes the price of nontradables to rise relative to the price of tradables forcing consumers to substitute the latter for the former. The net effect depends to a large extent on the two elasticities in that expression. Under these circumstances, it is most convenient to treat $\tilde{Q}_n$ as exogenous and to calculate the growth rates of the other two commodities, $\tilde{Q}_x$ and $\tilde{Q}_m$, on the basis of both $\tilde{Q}_n > 0$ and $\tilde{Q}_n < 0$. Therefore

$$\tilde{Q}_x = \frac{1}{|\lambda'|} [\{(\delta_L + \lambda_{Lx} + \lambda_{Lm})\lambda_{Tm} + \lambda_{Lm}\delta_T\}\tilde{b}_{Lt}$$

$$+ \lambda_{Tm}\lambda_{Ln}\tilde{b}_{Ln} + (\lambda_{Lm}\lambda_{Tn} - \lambda_{Ln}\lambda_{Tm})\tilde{Q}_n] \qquad (6.33)$$

$$\tilde{Q}_m = -\frac{1}{|\lambda'|} [\{(\delta_L + \lambda_{Lx} + \lambda_{Lm})\lambda_{Tx} + \lambda_{Lx}\delta_T\}\tilde{b}_{Lt}$$

---

[i]Use is made of equations (6.10), (6.12), (6.29) and (6.31) as well as the fact that the sum of the four elasticities in (6.28) is zero.

Table 6-1
Growth of the Outputs of Exportables and Importables Due to Growth of Labor Productivity

Change in the Output of Nontradables	Orderings of Labor Intensity		
	(1) $Q_x > Q_n > Q_m$	(2) $Q_n > Q_x > Q_m$	(3) $Q_x > Q_m > Q_n$
(i) $\tilde{Q}_n > 0$	$\tilde{Q}_x = ?, \tilde{Q}_m < 0$	$\tilde{Q}_x = ?, \tilde{Q}_m = ?$	$\tilde{Q}_x > 0, \tilde{Q}_m < 0$
(ii) $\tilde{Q}_n < 0$	$\tilde{Q}_x > 0, \tilde{Q}_m = ?$	$\tilde{Q}_x > 0, \tilde{Q}_m < 0$	$\tilde{Q}_x = ?, \tilde{Q}_m = ?$

$$+ \lambda_{Tx}\lambda_{Ln}\tilde{b}_{Ln} + (\lambda_{Lx}\lambda_{Tn} - \lambda_{Ln}\lambda_{Tx})\tilde{Q}_n] \tag{6.34}$$

where

$$|\lambda'| = \lambda_{Lx}\lambda_{Tm} - \lambda_{Tx}\lambda_{Lm} > 0$$

because, as in Chapter 2, the exportable commodity is assumed to be more labor intensive than the importable commodity.

If the last terms in both (6.33) and (6.34) are positive, then the exportable industry will expand while the importable industry will contract. But the sign of these terms depends on what is happening to the nontradable industry as well as the labor intensity of this industry vis-à-vis the two tradable industries. All the relevant possibilities are shown in Table 6-1.

Even by specifying the possible labor intensities and the change in output of nontradables, there are a number of cases where the growth of outputs of exportables and importables still cannot be determined. As Table 6-1 indicates, only in cases (i)(3) and (ii)(2) is this possible. In any case, total real output or income does in fact grow as shown by equation (6.31) because increasing labor productivity allows the transformation curve to move outward.

The Relationship Between Income and Private
Expenditures

In the static models of Chapters 4 and 5, wealth accumulation was assumed to involve lags and incomplete adjustment. In other words, total private expenditures (E) were determined by the level of money income (Y) and a proportion of the gap (if any) between desired wealth in this period and actual wealth in the last period. In an inflationary environment, it is more appropriate to assume that wealth holders anticipate the deterioration of their real wealth such that they make continuous and complete adjustments in their actual wealth accumulation to the ever-changing real wealth position. This proposition is caputred by the following equation:

$$E = Y - \overset{+}{\overline{W}} \tag{6.35}$$

while by definition

$$\dot{W} = Y - E \tag{6.36}$$

Combining these two equations proves equation (6.16) used above. The determination of desired wealth is still

$$\overline{W} = \mu Y \tag{6.37}$$

Taking time derivatives of (6.37) and substituting into (6.35) produces

$$E/Y = 1 - \mu \tilde{Y} \tag{6.38}$$

For stability, it is assumed that $0 < \mu \tilde{Y} < 1$. In equilibrium $\tilde{Y}$ is constant so that

$$\tilde{E} = \tilde{Y} \tag{6.39}$$

To the extent that desired wealth is growing during the inflationary process, private expenditures will be less than total income, the difference being saved, but the two variables grow at the same rate.

Conclusions

A small open economy will find that inflationary pressures generated abroad will be transmitted to the domestic commodity, factor, and asset markets. If the SOE maintains a fixed exchange rate, the authorities in the SOE will be powerless to influence this "imported inflation." If, on the other hand, they opt for a flexible exchange rate and are prepared to see it drift in the appropriate direction, then a rate of inflation different from that prevailing in the rest of the world can be maintained.[17]

It has been argued lately (most persuasively by Milton Friedman) that any rate of inflation is optimum as long as it is constant, because this reduces the chances of economic decisions being frustrated by unexpected changes in the rate of inflation and eliminates many of the "burdens" of inflation. In this regard, flexible exchange rates are to be preferred over fixed rates. To the extent that the world rate of inflation is not constant, but exhibits both upward and downward trends, the SOE can maintain a smooth inflationary path by allowing the exchange rate to appreciate at a faster pace whenever the world rate of inflation declines and by forcing the exchange rate to move in the opposite direction whenever the world rate of inflation is in an upturn. This is an advantage of more than minor significance.

Notes

1. A similar distinction is made by F. A. Lutz and Egon Sohmen, *How Can a Country Escape Imported Inflation?* Stuttgart and Mainz, W. Kohlhammer, Gmbh., 1965; S. I. Katz, "'Imported Inflation' and the Balance of Payments," *The Bulletin* of the Institute of Finance of the Graduate School of Business Administration, New York University, nos. 91-92, 1973.

2. R. W. Jones, "The Structure of Simple General Equilibrium Models," *Journal of Political Economy* 73 (1965): 557-72.

3. Ibid., p. 568.

4. See, for instance, W. L. Smith, *Macroeconomics*, Homewood, Ill., Richard D. Irwin, 1970, p. 359.

5. Milton Friedman, "The Role of Monetary Policy," *American Economic Review* 58 (1968): 1-17.

6. E. S. Phelps, "Money-Wage Dynamics and Labor Market Equilibrium," *Journal of Political Economy* 76 (1968): 678-711.

7. H. S. Houthakker, "An International Comparison of Household Expenditure Patterns," *Econometrica* 25 (1957): 532-51.

8. A. W. Phillips, "The Relation Between Unemployment and the Rate of Change of Wages in the United Kingdom, 1861-1957," *Economica*, n.s., 25 (1958): 283-99.

9. B. L. Scarfe, "A Model of the Inflation Cycle in a Small Open Economy," *Oxford Economic Papers* 25 (1973): 192-203.

10. Egon Sohmen, "The Effect of Devaluation on the Price Level," *Quarterly Journal of Economics* 72 (1958): 273-83.

11. R. I. McKinnon, *Monetary Theory and Controlled Flexibility in the Foreign Exchanges,* Essays in International Finance, no. 84, Princeton, Princeton University, 1971.

12. Ibid., p. 24.

13. This relationship assumes that changes in the rate of inflation leave the real rate of interest unaffected, representing the "Fisherian" approach to the determination of the nominal interest rate. See Irving Fisher, *The Theory of Interest*, New York, Augustus M. Kelley, 1961, Ch. II. However, it is possible that an increase in the rate of inflation will cause a higher nominal rate as well as a lower real rate. For a discussion of this possibility, see R. A. Mundell, "Inflation and Real Interest," *Journal of Political Economy* 71 (1963): 280-83.

14. Jones, "The Structure of Simple General Equilibrium Models," p. 568.

15. Ibid.

16. Ibid., p. 566.

17. Many of these conclusions are also derived by S. J. Turnovsky and André Kaspura, ''An Analysis of Imported Inflation in a Short-run Macroeconomic Model,'' *Canadian Journal of Economics* 7 (1974): 355-80. However, their model assumes that the price of the export good is determined in domestic markets, being equal to the price of nontradables, so that the country is only a price-taker in the market for importables.

Index

Index

About the Author

Martin F. J. Prachowny is associate professor of economics at Queen's University in Kingston, Ontario, Canada. He received his education at The University of Toronto and The University of Michigan. He is the author of *A Structural Model of the U.S. Balance of Payments* (North-Holland Publishing Company, 1969), a coeditor of *Bretton Woods Revisited* (University of Toronto Press, 1972), as well as a contributor to a number of professional journals.